How to . . .

D1085569

get the mos

COLES NOTES

Key Point
Basic concepts in point form.

Close Up
Additional hints, notes, tips or background information.

Watch Out!
Areas where problems frequently occur.

Quick Tip
Concise ideas to help you learn what you need to know.

Remember This!
Essential material for mastery of the topic.

How to . . .

Do a Great Job Interview

Interview preparation

Selling yourself

Common questions

and answers

COLES NOTES have been an indispensable aid to students on five continents since 1948.

COLES NOTES now offer titles on a wide range of general interest topics as well as traditional academic subject areas and individual literary works. All COLES NOTES are written by experts in their fields and reviewed for accuracy by independent authorities and the Coles Editorial Board.

COLES NOTES provide clear, concise explanations of their subject areas. Proper use of COLES NOTES will result in a broader understanding of the topic being studied. For academic subjects, Coles Notes are an invaluable aid for study, review and exam preparation. For literary works, COLES NOTES provide interesting interpretations and evaluations which supplement the text but are not intended as a substitute for reading the text itself. Use of the NOTES will serve not only to clarify the material being studied, but should enhance the reader's enjoyment of the topic.

© Copyright 1999 and Published by
COLES PUBLISHING. A division of Prospero Books
Toronto - Canada
Printed in Canada

Cataloguing in Publication Data
Bishop, Carol Anne, 1947–

How to—do a great job interview

(Coles notes) ISBN 0-7740-0588-2

1. Employment interviewing.   I. Title.   II. Series

HF5549.5.I6B57 1998   650.14   C98-930273-3

Publisher: Nigel Berrisford
Editing: Paul Kropp Communications
Book design and layout: Karen Petherick, Markham, Ontario

Manufactured by Webcom Limited
Cover finish: Webcom's Exclusive DURACOAT

Contents

CHAPTER ONE

Jobs and interviews in a changing work world

Thirty years ago, a person could enter the work force and literally do only a single job interview in an entire career. Fresh out of school, a young person might make such a convincing impression in that one interview that he or she would land the job, then proceed up the corporate ladder on the basis of performance and job evaluations.

How things have changed! Now we no longer talk about lifetime jobs or even lifetime careers. Many people change jobs every few years, and careers more than once or twice in a lifetime. Even advancement within a single company often means being inter-viewed by a new boss or team on a fairly regular basis. Many people today are not employed full-time but work at temporary or contract positions. Anyone in today's economy must plan to do a great job interview, not once or twice, but perhaps dozens of times during a working life.

Employers today are looking for people who demonstrate flexibility, talent, analytical and problem-solving abilities, excellent interpersonal skills, as well as broad technical abilities. These are known as employability or soft skills. Such skills share equal importance with hard technical skills acquired through further education, apprenticeship or on-the-job experience. Sophisticated interviewing techniques have been devised to detect these less-concrete soft skills in prospective employees.

It stands to reason that as more people go from job to job throughout their working lives, they will find themselves constantly in interview situations. Each project or mini-job will mean another

1

interview to prove your skills, expertise and experience. As a potential employee, you are selling or renting your unique talents. Since there will be lots of people out there offering their special services, your success rate depends on how well you sell yourself. Crass as it may seem, the employer is the customer and your skills and abilities are the product.

It is essential to keep in mind the purpose of any job interview. You are there to convince potential employers of their need for your services. It must never appear that you are there because you **need** the work.

Everyone can learn to do a great job interview, but many people simply don't bother to take the time to learn the techniques. Going into a situation unprepared and just flying by the seat of your pants simply doesn't work in a competitive employment environment. To make it a more level playing field, give yourself the best possible opportunity by being prepared. Preparation and practice lead to confidence – and confidence will land you a job.

Laying the groundwork is necessary long before you get to the actual interview itself. Begin the work by taking a complete and honest inventory of your skills and accomplishments. You need to know exactly what you can offer the employer and what skills you need to acquire through further training or experience. You have probably heard that expression – lifelong learning. With technology changing so rapidly, it is a game of constant catch-up. A Canadian survey revealed that nearly half the working population are busy upgrading by taking courses on their own time and at their own expense. If you haven't kept up-to-speed with the technological advances in your profession, it is simply self-defeating and demoralizing to place yourself in an interview where you have to admit you don't have the required qualifications.

Knowing yourself means going after work that you will enjoy and that you are qualified to do. But knowing yourself also means recognizing the many generic skills that you already possess. So often we fail to identify the unique skills or benefits we can offer to prospective employers. Before you ever get to the stage of looking for work, you need to spend the time to discover:

- who you are
- what you do
- what you can offer to a prospective employer

This book provides a step-by-step approach to dealing with all aspects of the interview process. After you have gained some experience you will be able to add your own personal knowledge to what makes a great interview for you. There is no single template for a great job interview.

Executive recruiters toss out the equation that a bad hire costs a company 10 times the salary of the person. So if the person's annual salary is $100,000, the mistake costs the corporation a million dollars. A book directed at interviewers warns that it costs approximately $5,000 to replace a clerical person and approximately $20,000 to replace a manager or professional person. Whatever the actual figures, you get the picture. Bottom line – no organization can afford to make the expensive mistake of hiring the wrong person for the job. They have done their homework to make their hiring decision as wisely as possible. By following the steps in this book, you will be ready to give them what they need to chose you.

CHAPTER TWO

Getting ready

You've landed that elusive job interview. You may feel it's time to let up and relax. You've worked hard developing your résumé and mailing copies out to targeted companies, networking, telephoning, searching want ads, surfing the Net and even visiting job marts. It's pay-off time. You've bagged an interview and know that your skills and experience perfectly match the job requirements.

Now is the time to kick into high gear and really start to work for that job or contract. The key is research: to know everything you possibly can about the business – even the whole industry – as well as the specific requirements for the position. You want to be as confident as possible during the interview. Being fully briefed gives you that confidence.

In today's highly competitive job market lots of people know that it is essential to do their homework before the job interview. It's now the norm. So don't assume that you will have the edge simply because you have done some research. It's the depth of your understanding of the company itself and the industry in general that will make you stand out from the other candidates. Go the extra mile in doing your research.

PHONE CALLS

Start with the obvious. Make a phone call to the company to see what documents they can provide: sales and marketing brochures, annual reports, copies of in-house newsletters. You should know everything you possibly can about the product or services of the organization. Often this material will provide you with the organization's mission statement. Think about that statement carefully. Picking up this material in person gives you the opportunity to get a feel for the lay of the land. You will know how to get there, be able to check out the dress code and get a sense of the atmosphere - fewer surprises on the day of the actual interview! Read the company newsletters carefully for possible information about the interviewer. There may be a feature article that gives clues about the interviewer's work philosophy or outside activities.

INTERNET

Also pay a visit to the company's Web site. There is a wealth of information to be found online. If you don't have access to the Internet at home, there are opportunities elsewhere. Most libraries offer Internet access; universities and community colleges are another possibility.

Along with the company's own homepage, there are literally hundreds of other potential Web sites for invaluable information. Two excellent books for more information on researching online are *Job-Hunting on the Internet,* by Richard Bolles, and *Get Wired, You're Hired,* by Canadian Internet specialist Mark Swartz.

Here are a few excellent Web sites to get you started:

Industry Canada
http://strategis.ic.gc.ca (1-800-328-6189 Help Desk for the Web site)
Provides industry profiles, key economic trends, export and import information.

CareerConnect - *The Globe and Mail*
http://www.theglobeandmail.com/careerconnect
Offers something for everyone. You can post your résumé (for a fee) or search for jobs using keywords. It has helpful articles and information on upcoming job fairs and useful associations.

 Across Canada, there are free walk-in Employment Resource Centers sponsored by Human Resources Development Canada. Here you can access the Internet as well as use many other services such as phones and fax machines, plus computers to write résumés.

THE LIBRARY

Go to the business section of the public library. You will be able to find information on all publicly held companies since they are required to file documents with the securities exchange commissions. Private companies without shareholders are not legally required to file public information documents, so the sleuthing may be more of a challenge. General business directories give you basic information such as a business's address, number of employees, line of business and perhaps annual sales figures. All of this will be useful in your job interview.

DIRECTORIES

There are a variety of business directories – both national and regional, general and specific industries.

The Blue Book of Canadian Businesses profiles leading Canadian companies. This is an excellent starting point. You can find information on parent and subsidiary companies, number of employees, nature of the business. It provides useful financial information including sales/revenue, net income, total assets. Sometimes, it includes the name and phone number of a person to contact for additional information.

Standard and Poor's Register of Corporations, Directors and Executives (3 vols.) lists the major United States corporations.

There are many specific sector directories such as:

Guide to the Canadian Financial Services Industry
Directory of Canadian Management Consultants
Directory of Canadian Associations
Directory of Retail Chains in Canada (2 vols.)
Directory of Restaurant and Fast Food Chains in Canada
Directory of Canadian Consulting Engineers
Scott's Industrial Series (5 regional vols.)
Thomas Register of American Manufacturers (27 vols.)

Check out the date of the directory to make sure that you have current information. Double-check names by making a phone call to confirm the facts.

Another valuable resource is *The Financial Post Investment Reports* which provides historical and current financial data for 500 Canadian public companies. These reports can be found in the business section of most large libraries.

ANNUAL REPORTS

Review annual reports with a healthy skepticism. Obviously these glossy publications give the directors a chance to put their best face forward to shareholders. But an annual report will give a general picture of the company's financial stability. Read between the lines to recognize what features they are proud of and promoting. Does the report talk about future plans? Does it give any clues to how it treats its employees? For example, a Canadian manufacturing company prominently featured a large picture of workers under the cutline *People make a difference* and stressed that a majority of the company's shares are owned by employees. It further indicated that the company's multicultural hiring practice encouraged the transfer of trained and experienced personnel to production facilities around the world. These are two very important pieces of information for the prospective employee.

Broaden your search by investigating competitors and looking at the health of the entire industry. You may be saving yourself the unpleasant surprise of finding out, **after** you get the job, that the company is facing a hostile take-over or that its product or service is becoming obsolete.

OTHER SOURCES

Flesh out your research by scanning databases such as the Canadian Index to find the most up-to-date details in newspaper and magazine articles. Look for the name of the company, profiles of prominent people in the organization, general articles on the state of the industry. You are very likely to find invaluable facts in these feature articles.

Do phone research. Look through the telephone directory to locate any associations or business organizations that may be able to provide further information. Talking to anyone you know who already works at the company is helpful. However, you will have to be careful to separate hearsay and gossip from factual information.

THE JOB AD ITSELF

It's essential to get as much detail as possible about the position itself. If the job has been advertised, carefully analyze every word used.

INVENTORY CONTROL MANAGER

Reporting to the Vice President Operations, you will be responsible for the implementation and maintenance of state-of-the-art processes in the area of Inventory Management.

THE SUCCESSFUL CANDIDATE WILL:

- Be results-oriented and self-directed to fulfill the company's objectives
- Have a university degree or have a college program in Inventory Management
- Possess a good knowledge of modern Inventory Management techniques, methods and practices
- Have three years' experience in the field of Inventory Management
- Have strong analytical, computer and communication skills

When you begin your analysis, ask yourself: Do I have all the requisite educational and work experience? (It may not be necessary to have every requirement, but be objective and assess the essential skills. Clearly, in this case the job requires a prior knowledge of inventory management.) What are the state-of-the-art processes in inventory management? Can I talk knowledgeably about them? What systems do they use now? What improvements could I suggest? Each requirement is a direct clue to what you will be asked in the interview. Your answers must demonstrate that you have what it takes to do the job.

If your interview is the result of unearthing a vacancy by networking or by phoning the company directly, see if there is a job description. In human resources circles, this is known as candidate specifications. It provides precise details of the skills, educational level, qualification and experience requirements.

Research questions

Keep in mind this basic list of questions whenever you are researching:

- Who is the company/organization?
- What do they do?
- What is their background/history?
- Where are they heading?
- What new products or services are in the works?

Then, make a list of your own personal concerns – both big and small.

- Is the location convenient?
- Is the salary range within my expectations?
- Does it seem like a place where I would be happy working?
- Will it enhance my career goals?

PRACTICE MAKES GREAT INTERVIEWS

Visualization is a popular tool in the personal growth movement. To visualize you simply clear your mind of everything else and imagine an experience in the most positive light. This technique can be used very effectively in preparing for a job interview. Visualize every step of the process from entering the office to making an effective closing statement.

After you have visualized, practice the whole procedure. Actually say your opening statement out loud, outlining your top three to five skills that mesh perfectly with the job requirements. Practice answers to cover all categories of frequently asked questions. Inject a little humor. Enjoy yourself. Yes, you are talking to yourself – perhaps even chuckling at times – but this is the best practice.

Now, get someone to role-play with you. Make sure your partner is a sympathetic and supportive friend. You may hate rehearsing with an audience, but it is the most effective way of polishing your interview techniques. Let your partner randomly ask you some of the frequently asked sample questions from this book. If a potential prime minister can spend the time practicing and role-playing before debates, surely you don't have to feel silly preparing for your next job.

It is highly effective if you can videotape your job-interview rehearsal. In reviewing the tape, don't cringe at your distracting mannerisms. Be gentle with yourself. Use the tape as a constructive opportunity to correct and polish your job interview performance. Pay particular attention to your voice. Do you tend to rush your words or get high-pitched when tense? Watch your body language. Is there a little nervous tic that you have not been aware of? Do you have a nervous giggle? Do you tend to stare disconcertingly? Or blink? Did you remember to smile occasionally?

Professional employment services, courses offered through government employment centers and career counseling services at universities and community colleges offer opportunities to practice with videotaped interviews.

BE PREPARED

Don't sabotage yourself by getting this far with research and rehearsal and then let up. You still have another crucial step before the interview itself – that's getting ready. Consider it a dress rehearsal or a time to check out the props. Make sure that the outfit you plan to wear is clean, all buttons secure. If you are scrambling around at the last minute, buttons will fly off and belts will go missing. Don't be like one young student who didn't do a dress rehearsal and realized at the last moment that he had left his dress shoes at a friend's house. He was left with the choice of sandals or beat-up running shoes. (Needless to say, the interview team wasn't impressed.)

On the day of your job interview, make sure you pack your briefcase with all of the following:

- extra copies of your résumé. You can refer to a copy during the interview to make sure to cover all the skills you want to stress. Offer to leave a fresh copy at the end of the interview.
- note book and pens. Jot down very brief notes. In particular, make note of any recommendations of courses for upgrading, professional associations to join and useful contact names.
- your business card. In business, there is often a ritual of presenting business cards at the beginning or end of a meeting.
- sample portfolio of work. Professions such as graphic artists, journalists, architects, art directors, interior decorators, and photographers will have samples of previous work projects. It's advisable not to leave your portfolio behind in case it becomes misplaced or, even worse, an unscrupulous person has the opportunity to copy your ideas.

On time

Think beforehand. Be kind to yourself by anticipating everything. Things will be tough enough without getting all flustered and unfocused because you have rushed in late.

- a separate sheet listing names, titles and contact numbers of your references. Be sure to alert your references after an interview to expect a phone call.

Have the name and title of the interviewer (make sure you know the correct pronunciation of the name), the exact directions with address, floor level and any instructions you have been given about parking arrangements. Most importantly, have the telephone number in case of a dreaded emergency which might make you late for the interview. Include your research notes about the job and the company to read on the bus or in a coffee shop. If driving, check that you have enough gas in the car and money for parking.

CHAPTER THREE

Dress for interview success

In today's workplace there are no hard and fast rules about the dress code. In some ways it was much easier when there was a strict list of do's and don'ts about dressing for a job interview. Looking at it positively, it means that today there's less chance of a social faux pas in your choice of clothes. While the staff members may be casually dressed, the job applicant is often expected to dress slightly more conservatively for the interview process.

As part of your preliminary research, it is essential to get a sense of what will be the most suitable attire for any particular interview. This can be done by visiting the location prior to the meeting to observe how the employees are dressed. Even better, phone the receptionist or someone in the human resources office to ask what is the appropriate dress style. Is it business formal or business casual? **Business formal** is a known quantity – for men, suits, long-sleeve dress shirts, brown or black leather shoes, ties in subdued colors. (For some inexplicable reason in the executive world, short-sleeve dress shirts are sneered at – Dilbert wears one.) For women, suits or tailored dresses with a jacket, pumps, simple jewelry and neutral-colored pantyhose. Smart women carry an extra pair of pantyhose because they have a nasty habit of running at the most inopportune moments. Never overdo the jewelry or make-up, less is best.

But what does **business casual** mean? And does it mean the same in all parts of the country? Is East Coast casual the same as West Coast casual? Generally speaking, business casual for men suggests a sports jacket, chino or other casual pants, polo shirts,

13

loafers or more casual lace-ups. For women, it means comfortable, flat loafers rather than high-heel pumps, smart sport skirts or pants and more laid-back accessories. In most corporate environments, it doesn't mean T-shirts with slogans, track pants, cut-offs or running shoes. Some of the more staid organizations still frown on jeans. But in other job cultures – the film and TV world, advertising, computer software – jeans may be the team uniform. It's up to you to check out the scene ahead of time. For the job interview, always dress somewhat conservatively. You can wear the company "uniform" once you're on the team.

Just to complicate the issue – many companies with a business-formal dress code now have dress-down days. This may be a regular day of the week or more sporadic – sometimes casual days are used as fundraisers. Even if your interview is on a casual day, dress more formally. However, if you have done your research and know that your interview is on a dress-down day, you won't be nonplussed by the more casually dressed interviewer. You can use the situation as a great ice breaker. For example, if you see a sign in the reception area stating it's a fundraising Casual Day for the United Way, you can say, "I see that XYZ company supports charities – that's great." It proves that you are observant and puts everyone at ease if the styles of dressing clash.

Check points for interview success

- clean, groomed hair
- clean and cut fingernails
- polished shoes
- no strong cologne/aftershave/perfume
- no sun/tinted glasses
- no garish, distracting jewelry

Another growing trend in larger companies is "business-appropriate attire" which translates as wearing the clothes suitable for the work that particular day. If it's a day of paperwork, casual wear is fine. But if it's a day of making customer calls, it's business formal. What is considered business appropriate attire for the interview? If in doubt, go the conservative route.

If you are a more experienced job-seeker, it is very important to be dressed in a contemporary style, but one that allows you still to feel like yourself. The classics never fail. There is nothing more obvious than someone trying to dress younger than they are. It's a good idea to cull through your wardrobe to weed out dated clothes. It's false economy to save a sports jacket you've always loved if it makes you stand out as yesterday's man. Likewise, entry-level job interviewees may have to invest in a few clothes more suitable to the workplace than the campus.

Carrying an attaché or briefcase denotes professionalism and seriousness. You can use it to carry a notebook and extra copies of your résumé. Women should chose either a briefcase or a handbag. Avoid having extra stuff in plastic bags. The key is to limit the clutter you are carrying. And recent graduates: leave your backpack at home. Save it for exploring the Himalayas; it leaves a bad impression at IBM or Cantel.

Often tips on dressing for the interview include the most obvious of suggestions – have clean hair, don't have body odor, have shiny shoes, don't chew gum. Common sense prevails. Overpowering perfume or aftershave, the clinging odor of cigarette smoke, the aroma of garlic are obviously offensive. Excellent personal hygiene, clothes that are not distracting and that are suitable for the time of day are self-evident. If you have any doubts about your own sense of appropriateness, ask a clothes-savvy friend for an honest opinion of your interview outfit.

There's that old adage – if you already look the part, you have more of a chance of getting the job. Dressing appropriately is one very simple and easy way to improve your chance of success. Perfectly qualified and competent job candidates in glaringly wrong outfits simply shoot themselves in the foot.

When you are making your notes after an interview, jot down what you wore. Often the job process requires a number of interviews and some of the same people may be present. Variety rather than the same "interview uniform" provides freshness and vitality to your presentation.

BODY LANGUAGE

Just as important as the clothes you wear is the way you present yourself – body language. There's no point getting tied up in knots about body language, but keep these few points in mind. First impressions count. Walk into the interviewer's office, standing straight and looking confident. Offer a dry, firm handshake. Don't get excited. Let the interviewer indicate where you are to sit. Think of how you are sitting – straight, but relaxed, arms in a natural position. Clasping your hands together or crossing your arms suggests you are uneasy or anxious (which may well be the case). Do a self-check to make sure you are not unconsciously fidgeting or jingling the change in your pocket. No hyperactive finger-tapping. Make eye contact but not with an unblinking stare, (but be sensitive to the fact that people in some cultures are uncomfortable with direct eye contact). If you are being interviewed by more than one person, include everyone in your gaze. Breathe. Above all, don't forget to occasionally smile.

Accepting a beverage during an interview can lead to problems. If everyone else is sipping coffee, you may be tempted to join the group. On the other hand, if you are the least bit accident-prone, it can prove a disaster. If you are relaxed or it seems comfortable, by all means accept their hospitality. But a gracious decline of "No thanks, I just had a cup of coffee before I came" gets you off the hook.

THE INTERVIEW STARTS AT THE DOOR

Show-time begins the moment you arrive at the organization. That means the parking lot attendant and the receptionist deserve the same respectful treatment as the person doing the interview. You might be standing in the elevator with one of the interviewers. You may be "Joe Cool" walking into the interview room, but if you were a bundle of nerves riding up the elevator, your cover is blown.

A vice president of a small manufacturing company chuckles as he relates how his office in an ultramodern black glass building looks out onto the path leading from the parking lot. Tense candidates pulling at their clothes or making odd facial gestures don't realize that he can see out from this non-reflecting black glass.

Give yourself ample time to get to the interview. It's a good idea to arrive at the building early, but not actually go in until closer to the hour of the interview. The pressure's off – everything is under control. You won't be late. Take the extra time to review your notes in a coffee shop or sitting in your car. In the winter months, give yourself enough time to get rid of bulky coat and boots. (Don't forget to bring your shoes: wearing wet outdoor boots or worse still, being forced to be in stocking feet, puts you at a serious disadvantage.) Visit the restroom to check out your appearance and dry your hands if you are nervously perspiring. Again, keep in mind that your interviewer may have also popped into the restroom and might be sharing the hand dryer with you.

Resist any temptation to babble in the reception area. Use this opportunity to observe everything around you. There may be some displayed promotional material or industry-related magazines to read. Often manufacturers display their products in the waiting-room area. If you are kept waiting, avoid clock-watching or openly showing your displeasure or impatience.

CHAPTER FOUR

It's a selling game: open, probe, close

At a job interview - like it or not - your task is to sell yourself. Interviewers facing you across the desk have three basic concerns:

- Who are you?
- What can you do for us?
- How much will it cost us to get your services?

The whole purpose of the job-interview exercise is to address those three concerns and prove that you are the best choice to supply the company's needs. Along with those three key questions, interviewers have lots of other smaller worries swirling around in their minds:

- Do you have the training required to do the job?
- How is your health? Will you take much time off?
- Do you really understand the reality of the demands of this job - the amount of travel, weekend overtime?
- Are you punctual and reliable?
- How stable is your home life?
- How will you fit into the company culture?
- Are you after my job?

It is your job to allay such employer fears. They are looking at you as an investment. You want to prove that your value exceeds their costs in hiring you.

In your role as a salesperson during the interview, it is essential to keep your customer's needs in mind. The employer is the customer. Your skills and experience are the commodity being sold.

Right off the mark, you need to make sure that the opening question gives you an opportunity to outline the benefits in hiring you.

OPEN

Salespeople today are taught to be customer-focused – meeting needs and overcoming objections. This is often referred to as the win-win model. In this new consultative sales model, the first and most important step is trust or rapport building. We have already discussed body language, the importance of first impressions. Walk into the interview with confidence, smile, offer a firm, dry handshake, make eye contact and wait to be seated. The rapport built in the first five minutes usually continues through the rest of the interview. At the first suitable moment, make your opening statement. Try to include the interviewer's name, your appreciation for the interview and an indication that you are ready to co-operate: "Mr. Brown, thank you for allowing me an interview with you today. I hope you get to know me and my skills." If the interviewer does not put you at ease with a little social banter, don't get tense. Take a moment to compose yourself. Don't feel compelled to fill the silence by blurting out that you didn't sleep very well last night or by making some ingratiating comment on the interviewer's tie. Silence is a potent tactic which is used by some interviewers to catch people off-guard.

During the interview, you are showing the benefits of choosing you over the other candidates. The focus for both you and employers is on **their** needs. You can see why it is essential to discover in advance through your investigation exactly what skill sets are required to do that specific job. It's not good enough to just know what you can do, the key is to know what you can do *for them*.

PROBE

After making an effective opening, the next stage in sales strategy is the **probe**. Probing is basically asking a few essential questions to uncover the customer's needs. Hopefully you already know most of the customer's needs through your research. The probe is also the time to deal with the employer's doubts. It means listening for both the direct question and the hidden agenda that may be behind it.

How can you be asking probing questions? Isn't the whole point of an interview to probe you? Well yes, but you can usually fit in a few questions yourself at the appropriate times. These questions should be cleverly worded to highlight information you want to get across to the interviewer. Probe to find out more about the employer's needs and you'll have an excuse to showcase yourself.

Never ask basic questions about the company: "How many employees does XYZ company have?" It only proves that you haven't done your basic research. But do ask a question to show that you have done your homework: "I noticed in reading your annual report that you will be expanding into the Far East market. When do you plan to begin implementing your market strategy?"

You may be able to do this probing at suitable moments throughout the course of the interview. However, if it is apparent that the interviewer sees your questions as annoying interruptions, save your probe until the appropriate time. It is a common practice to ask applicants near the end of the interview if they have any questions.

The initial interview is definitely not the time to ask "What's in it for me" questions such as:

- How much holiday time will I get?
- What are the working hours?
- How long is lunch break?
- What is the benefit package?
- What is the salary?

These are all very legitimate concerns and you will need to address them. However, this is not the appropriate moment. Those questions can be asked when you have been offered the position and are negotiating the terms of your employment.

Do ask questions dealing with the specific job. Word them to make the subtle assumption that you are a strong contender.

- What would be the first project I would be working on?
- Who would be my co-workers?
- Who would I report to?
- What opportunities will there be for more training?
- How much travel will be involved?

These types of positive inquiries make you sound confident and at the same time give you valuable information about the job. After all, you may finally decide that you don't want to take it, even if it is offered.

There is a delicate balance in asking questions. It is a mistake to challenge interviewers or make them feel defensive. This is not the time to dazzle by asking highly technical questions to prove your expertise. (Frequently you'll just display how shallow your own knowledge is.)

Ask a question if you see that the interviewer or panel has lost interest in your answer. This means always being aware of unspoken language – that glazed look of sheer boredom on the interviewer's face. Don't continue to blather on. Save the situation by stopping and asking, "Is this the type of information you are looking for?"

Occasionally you will come across a situation in which an unskilled interviewer does a monologue and never asks any questions. This happened to a woman who found herself being interviewed by a bitter ex-employee of the Canadian Broadcasting Corporation who talked on and on about the demise of public broadcasting. Although she had landed another job, this self-absorbed woman had completely forgotten that her purpose was to conduct a job interview. If you realize that you are being ineptly interviewed and so far haven't been asked any questions to give you an opportunity to sell your skills, it's time to step in. It may be possible to diplomatically interrupt by saying, "That's really interesting and I think my extensive desktop computer skills are just what you need to get new product information out to your clients."

Another function of the sales probe is to overcome doubts. The technique involves acknowledging that there is a concern. "I can understand your possible worry about my having two preschool children. You may be wondering if my parental responsibilities will interfere with my ability to work overtime. My husband works from home as a freelancer, but is also the primary caretaker of our children. We made that decision to allow me to work the necessary overtime which we know this position will require." You then follow up with the question: "Does that satisfy your concern about my ability to take on overtime or weekend work?" Human rights legislation makes many questions illegal. However, if there is an unspoken issue that may jeopardize your chance, this is your opportunity to confront it.

CLOSE

The **close** is the time to review the previously discussed benefits – namely your skills – and discuss the next step in the process. When it becomes clear that the interview is nearing an end, it's time to briefly restate your best three to five skills. These should be the ones that directly meet the employer's needs. It's a good idea to have a small file card on which you've written out the skills you have to offer which you want to discuss during the interview. Make a mental checkmark as you cover each one of them. Review that list at the end of the close and include any that were missed during the interview process.

For example, suppose you are being interviewed for a part-time retail sales position and you realize that you've come to the close without the interviewer asking about your familiarity with the equipment. There are many candidates for this sought-after job and you need to stress why you are the best choice: "I would just like to add that I am completely familiar with the cash register you have as well as debit and credit card procedures, so I can be on the floor selling from the day I start working for you." This is a cost-saving benefit to the employer. If you had left without letting the employer know you can fulfill this need – selling the products immediately – you would be one of many prospective candidates. This extra information may just tip the job in your direction.

As difficult as it may be for you to do, always remember to ask for the job. It's essential. Make it clear that you are interested in the position: "I've enjoyed this opportunity to talk with you and find out more details about the position. I think I have a lot to offer and would very much like to take on the challenge."

Politely, but not effusively, thank the interviewer or panel for taking the time with you. Keep making that eye contact and remember to smile. Show enthusiasm.

Try to discover the timeline for the hiring decision. Are there many more candidates to be interviewed? Who will be making the final decision? Ask permission to follow up with a phone call: "I very much enjoyed our conversation. Can I phone you in a week's time to follow up?" Don't prolong your exit. And just as you were aware of your body language as you entered the room, leave with the same sense of confidence. Make sure to take everything with you including notebook and briefcase. It is not impressive to come sheepishly back into the room to collect forgotten items.

What to leave behind

- Your business card (You can make them on a computer if the cost of professionally printed cards is beyond your means.)
- A fresh copy of your résumé (A health executive knocked the socks off her interview panel by leaving behind for each member a handsomely bound copy of her presentation with a cover page including her name, contact number and the date of the interview. She got the job.)
- List of references with telephone and fax numbers (Only if asked for. Phone your references immediately to advise them to expect a call.)

What to take away

- Business cards of interviewers (It is important to follow up with thank-you letters.)
- Additional documents such as in-house reports or materials you may have been asked to review
- Clear understanding of the job and the company's expectations
- A good sense of the company culture
- The commitment for you to be able to follow up with a phone call

CHAPTER FIVE

Types of interviews

You have to be ready to deal with many different kinds of interviews in today's competitive and complex job world. You may find yourself in a video or telephone-conference interview with a prospective employer half a world away. Soon you can expect a preliminary interview with a floppy disk. You pop the disk into your own personal computer, answer all the questions and E-mail it back. You may have to deal with a group of people all asking questions or spend an exhausting day bounced from person to person in the same corporation. You may be asked improbable questions, like "How many gas stations are there in the world?", on face tests that seem unrelated to the job. What's going on? Along with everything else in the employment world, the interview itself is changing.

Forewarned is forearmed. If you recognize that you are in a "behavior-style interview," you'll know that you are expected to show by examples of your past behavior how you are likely to perform in the future. You'll know they want stories. If the person is being unbearably rude, you may be in the midst of the "stress-style" interview. Then you will have to keep your cool at all costs. The point is to be aware and prepared for all possibilities.

ON-CAMPUS RECRUITERS AND JOB MARTS

These are large, impersonal situations rather like cattle-call auditions for actors. Fewer companies these days need to seek out prospective employees on campus. However, recruiters from large multinational corporations still target outstanding graduates at the top universities. Often they know ahead of time the candidates they are interested in meeting. Then they sponsor a social event in which recruiters work the crowd to inspect graduates. If you find yourself making seemingly small talk with a campus recruiter, know that you are being checked out for your communication and interpersonal skills. You are already in an interview!

JOB MARTS/FAIRS

Job marts or fairs (sometimes called career exchanges) are opportunities for a number of companies in the same industry to scout out prospective employees. These job fairs are popular with high-tech industries. Usually in hotels, representatives from numerous companies set up booths or rooms. The job-seeker usually just gets the chance to submit a résumé and collect general information. Your goal at the job fair is to get to the next stage of an interview at the company premises. Richard Bolles, whose book *What Color Is Your Parachute?* has been the bestselling job-hunting book for over 25 years, rates job fairs as the "most ineffective" way to approach large organizations. He gives you a zero to eight percent chance of actually landing an interview with a decision-maker. Bolles may be right. Certainly it's true that the main function of job-fair recruiters is to screen out people. However if you believe in the "leave no stone unturned" job search theory, you might consider attending a job fair – if only for the experience. It helps to check out in advance if there is a list of the companies represented at the fair. There is often additional information on advertised Web sites.

SCREEN-OUT INTERVIEWS

The sole purpose of this type of interview is to exclude everyone but the few with the required qualifications. This will very likely be conducted by a recruiter or human resources professional. It's a highly impersonal experience in which you will be skilfully quizzed to validate all the information on your résumé. It's a time for giving just the facts. Save the stories and examples for the decision-making interviewer. If you are uncertain as to whether this is just a preliminary screen-out meeting, tactfully ask for an explanation of the selection procedure.

SELECTION INTERVIEWS

In mid-sized to large organizations with personnel or human resources departments, you will find yourself going through a two-step process. If you make it through the screening-out stage, you move on to the selection interview. It may be with just a single manager or supervisor, or with a number of senior executives. If it is a small or owner-run business, you go right into the hiring interview. These hiring or selection interviews will vary in format.

One-on-One: This is the traditional two-party interview. These one-on-one's are still the norm. The interview process may consist of talking only to one person or having a series of one-on-one interviews. The questioner may use any or all of the interview styles: be highly structured and experienced or conversational and intuitive. If the interviewer is the person you will ultimately be reporting to, he or she is likely trying to assess how you will fit into the team.

Panel: It is preferable to find out in advance who and how many people will be at the interview. But don't show visible surprise if you are ushered into a room with more than one interviewer. Keep your composure. In a not-for-profit organization, it may be members of the board. Or it may be a cross-section of people you would be working with in a large organization. The panel interview becomes more common as the level of your career advances. One panel member may be the ultimate decision-maker and not necessarily be the person who does much of the questioning. The panel interview tests your social skills in dealing with a group of people. Be sure to make eye contact with everyone in the room. It's human nature to focus on a sympathetic person or someone you have met before, but keep your eyes moving to all the faces. When a question is being asked, direct your gaze to the person asking the question. At the end of the interview, thank the group for seeing you and, if appropriate, shake hands all around.

SERIES OF INTERVIEWS

This is more often used for entry and middle level job applicants by large organizations. Over a single day, the candidate meets with several people, one after another. They may all ask very different questions or there may be repetition. This can be a tiring experience and the trick is to keep the answers fresh and enthusiastic for each interviewer. The group gets together later to discuss your overall performance and to make the final decision. At that point, you may be asked back on another day for a final interview. Keep up your stamina – a good job is worth it.

THE MEALTIME INTERVIEW

There can be any number of reasons why you might be invited for a dining-out interview. It may be a matter of convenience – you are meeting someone who is recruiting while in town on other business. Or it may be a very deliberate tactic to examine your social graces. Pitfalls are everywhere with the mealtime interview. As a rule of thumb, take your cue from the interviewer. Select a meal of comparable value. Obviously don't choose something overly messy or distracting. Spaghetti is nearly always a mistake, soup can be a disaster and some vegetarians can't abide the smell of meat. Always give liver and other kinds of edible offal a pass! Although appearing appreciative of the meal, focus your complete attention on the conversation.

To drink or not to drink, that is always the question. The answer is that it's a judgment call. Mineral water is a fail-safe solution. Never order a drink if the interviewer is not drinking. And never order more that one drink under any circumstances. Keep your wits about you.

COMPUTER-ASSISTED INTERVIEW

Imagine walking into a situation where you are asked to sit at a computer and answer a series of questions – anywhere from 50 to over a 100 multiple-choice questions touching on your general background, skills, employment history and educational qualifications. This technique is popular with hotel chains, hospitals and retailers who are required to be constantly interviewing large numbers of people. Often these computer questionnaires are matched to hard-copy job applications which you have been asked to fill out earlier. The two documents are compared to detect inconsistencies in your answers. As well, these programs are often set up to check out other aspects, such as how long you took to answer specific questions.

TELEPHONE/TELECONFERENCING INTERVIEW

Picture answering an ad in an international publication and suddenly finding yourself in a telephone interview with someone half a world away. This preliminary interview may lead to you jetting to another continent for a follow-up interview. This was the experience of a Toronto-based MBA graduate with five years' international banking experience who answered an advertisement in the *Financial Times*. He was screened in a telephone interview by a recruiter in Germany, flown to Frankfurt and landed a lucrative job in the company's branch office in Kiev, Ukraine. The initial phone call was conducted in German, a language in which the candidate had stated he had a fluency. The answers he gave in his telephone interview convinced the company to go to the considerable expense of flying him to Germany where he was involved in a strenuous round of face-to-face interviews.

If the interview is via a long-distance call, don't fall into the trap of rushing because it's expensive. It's the company's money, after all.

In most circumstances – be it a long-distance or local call – telephone interviews are a screening-out process. Once you have sent out a résumé, be prepared for an unexpected telephone interview. If the call has come at the worst possible moment (your toddler is throwing a tantrum or you are standing stark naked and dripping wet from the shower), make arrangements to call back as soon as possible. If it's a favorable time to pursue the interview, be prepared by having a file with all the company research and a copy of your cover letter nearby. Some points to keep in mind:

- Get rid of any background noise such as the radio or an operating dishwasher.
- Hold the receiver properly so you are not doing a heavy breathing routine or your answers are indistinct.

- Listen very, very carefully to what you are being asked. Don't be afraid to ask the person to repeat the question.
- Don't interrupt.
- Take notes of the key points in the conversation.

Don't fall into the trap of becoming chatty. Remember this is a formal job interview. Make it your objective to get to the next stage of a face-to-face interview. At the end of any telephone interview, politely thank the person for phoning you and, if appropriate, say you look forward to meeting them in person. Take down all the details for the upcoming meeting – time, date, address (any special instructions on the location) and who will be at the interview.

 If you are conducting a job search and anticipating a number of telephone interviews, it might be worthwhile to consider investing in Call Display, the system which shows the name of the person/company dialing in. This would ensure you had advance warning and could be prepared and professional on answering the call. Other family members would also be forewarned of the importance of the caller.

VIDEO-CONFERENCING INTERVIEW

This is an "out-of-body" experience in which you are placed alone in a room with a camera and expected to relate to people thousands of miles away. The alienated feeling is compounded by the fact that there is usually a slight time lag in the connection (like a bad long-distance telephone conversation). Unless you have had professional training in this type of situation, it does not show you to your advantage. However, if you keep calm, don't wildly gesticulate and answer the questions as you would in a face-to-face interview, you will be fine. In our global economy these video-conferencing interviews are becoming more common.

INFORMATION-ONLY INTERVIEW

This is a very different type of interview – a fact-finding or fishing expedition. As a proactive job seeker, you have secured an appointment with a busy, but agreeable person to find out the job potential both within that company and the industry itself. This is not a job interview. But it may lead to several job interviews.

Since the person has kindly agreed to see you, make sure not to waste a minute of his or her time. You set the agenda in this type of interview. Open by thanking the person for the opportunity and propose the length of time you will be taking: "I realize that you are extremely busy and I would like to talk to you for 20 minutes." Check for acceptance: "Is this okay with you?" Once you have established the time frame, stick to it. Don't waste time by asking for information that you can easily find out yourself with research. The purpose of the session is to network and glean insider tips. Prepare your questions in advance to optimize the time. But don't get so caught up in trying to get answers to every question that you forget to listen. Track very carefully what the person is telling you and follow up potential leads.

Here is a sample of the types of questions you can ask in an information-only interview:

- What developments on the horizon could affect future opportunities?
- Is there job potential in the industry?

- What types of skills and knowledge are required to do this type of work?
- Are there certain personality traits that make it easier to do the work in this field?
- Can you recommend any courses I should take before proceeding further with my job search?
- What positions does my current experience qualify me for?
- What companies might be interested in hiring someone with my background?
- Are there professional associations I should join?
- Can you see any objections or reservations an employer may have with my current qualifications?
- Could you describe a typical workday for me?
- Is it possible to have a tour of the facilities and see the work being done here?
- What is the normal salary range in this line of work?
- Is there anything else you think I need to know? Who else would you recommend I speak with? When I call, may I use your name?
- What do you think of my résumé? How would you suggest I change it?

Rather than doing rapid-fire questions, allow the person to talk about personal experiences within the industry. For example, ask her how she got her job or what motivates her, if she was starting over again, would she do anything differently? The fact that the person agreed to meet with you indicates a willingness to share and help you in your job search.

If it is appropriate, ask for the opportunity to take a tour of the facility. Likely it will not be the busy executive who gives you the tour, but the information you receive will still be valuable. Observe and ask questions. This is an excellent opportunity to get a better understanding of particular job requirements. You may recognize that people are working with a computer program unfamiliar to you. Make a mental note to get up-to-speed with that particular program. And be sure to thank your guide for taking the time to show you around.

If the person recommends changes to your résumé, be sure to send a revised copy. Needless to say, send a thank-you letter. If you think it suitable and have the means, you might consider sending a small plant or other appropriate token to express your appreciation.

 Never ask directly for a job in an information-only interview. This was not the purpose of the meeting and it is an abuse of the interviewee's generosity in meeting with you. However it is fair to ask to be "kept in mind" or for your name to be passed on to someone else in the industry who might be interested in your qualifications.

Styles of interviews

Every interview is a unique situation. You may find yourself dealing with the embarrassed ramblings of a person who hasn't a clue about talking to a prospective employee or facing a human resources specialist with a polished information-gathering agenda.

While each interviewer has his/her individual approach, there are several quite distinctive interview styles. Over time you will gain experience in recognizing them. It may not be immediately apparent if the interview is being conducted according to a set style or if it is a composite style, but there are clues to alert you to the general approach of each interviewer. Each approach calls for a different strategy on your part.

BEHAVIOR-BASED INTERVIEWS

The current trend in human resources is the behavior-based (sometimes called competency-based) interview. The theory is that people's behavior is based on habit, so how we have reacted in past job situations is a clear indication of how we will react in the future.

The tip-off of a behavior based interview is if you are asked to describe a scenario in which you were required to solve a past problem. Questions that begin "What did you do?" or "Tell me about a time ..." should be a flag that you are in the midst of a behavior-based interview. You can plan ahead of time for this type of interview by preparing several concrete examples from your past experiences. You will already have several of these answers prepared if you have prepared a résumé which includes a selection of accomplishments or achievements. Use these examples to expand upon and rehearse. Don't recite a memorized tale. Be conversational, anecdotal. Make the story interesting – yes even amusing – and make sure it shows you in the best possible light.

If you are an entry level job seeker, don't begin by apologizing for a lack of experience. Use non-work or part-time work training to provide a story. Let's say you are looking for your first job after getting your degree in social work and you don't have any direct field experience. You are asked, "What did you do when a client was disruptive?" You could relate how you dealt with a ratty little kid when you were a day camp counselor. Your answer would illustrate that you understand the problem-solving skills they are looking for and how you handled a comparable conflict-resolution situation.

SCENARIO-BASED INTERVIEWS

While the behavior-based style interview focuses on how you have handled professional situations in the past, the scenario-based interview deals with how well you cope in the present. There are two basic variations – the **simulation** and the **situational interview.**

Another name for the **simulation** interview is role playing. The idea of being put on the spot to role play gives many job-seekers nightmares. However, if suddenly confronted with this scenario, take a deep breath and accept the challenge. A favorite approach by interviewers is to ask the candidate to suddenly become a salesperson. For example, let's says the interviewer holds up his coffee mug and says, "Sell this mug to me." After taking a few seconds to collect your thoughts, you take the plunge. "Along with its attractive design, this dishwasher proof and break-resistant mug is exceptionally functional. The larger-sized handle is easy for everyone to hold comfortably. It's stackable and therefore takes up little room in small office kitchens." Then pause and close by asking, "How many would you like to order?" This simple selling exercise tests how quickly you think on your feet and the scope of your communications skills. It often pays to have such a spiel ready.

One social service agency asks potential candidates to take part in a role-playing scenario in which they are watched as they handle a phone call. A staff member (phoning from another room) poses as a distraught client in a crisis situation. The candidate is observed as he/she fields the call and deals with the emergency. A cool head is needed, not only to handle the caller, but because you are being observed in the process.

The other variation is the **situational** format in which you are presented with a hypothetical situation and asked to solve the issue. For example, here is a scenario presented to candidates for a position as a human resources coordinator. It concerns a painful downsizing decision reducing the staff by one senior secretary. You are told:

"All three of the present senior secretaries are good performers. Senior secretary #1 has been with the Center the longest (11 years). Senior secretary #2 has been in the position for three years, but has more than eight years of service as a secretary at the Center. Her current boss considers her a real crackerjack who is 100 percent committed to the work of the Center and who is always ready to go the extra mile. Senior secretary #3 has been with the Center for more than seven years and she too, is known for her commitment, reliability, ability and willingness to work extra hours.

"The Center prides itself on making 'fair' decisions. It values longevity of service and staff who demonstrate commitment to the values of the Center (accessibility, accountability, efficiency, effectiveness, responsiveness, respectfulness, flexibility and commitment to continuity of service). The reduction of three senior secretaries to two, is the only downside to the decision to consolidate.

"As an HR practitioner, what are some of the things you would suggest that Senior Management should consider in order to resolve this situation, to everyone's satisfaction, if possible?"

In this particular case, the candidates were allowed to give written solutions to this problem, a task we won't attempt here. But the basic concept remains: for senior-level jobs, be prepared for the presentation of a difficult situation and be ready to say how you would deal with it.

CONVERSATIONAL INTERVIEWS

In the conversational style, the interviewer is using rapport to get the information she wants. You are being encouraged to reveal yourself. Go ahead and reveal – but just be acutely aware of exactly what you are saying. Unlike the behavior-based interview with its tip-off "Tell me about a time ...?" format, there is no specific clue to indicate that you are in a conversational-style interview. However as time goes on and you continue to feel as if you are chatting, you know that is the style. Never forget that the person "just chatting" with you is fact-finding. A job interview is never a friendly talk between two equals. As always, the interviewer is the customer and you are the seller.

The skilled interviewer often uses a conversational interview in a purposeful, structured manner with a very specific agenda. On the other hand, this may indicate that the person has no training in the interview process and no focus or purpose. One zany television series had the memorable scene of a lecherous TV news director interviewing candidates for the position of researcher. The news director amiably chats about his love of skiing with an attractive ski bunny. After a long, rambling tête-a-tête he winds up the interview by tossing out the question: "Oh, have you any experience as a researcher?" "No, is that a problem?" replies the ski bunny. "No, no," the news director quickly responds. It's a hilarious scene and hopefully not a norm in the real world. But there are occasions when the interviewer is inept and never gets around to asking you any questions. Don't lose sight of the purpose of a job interview. Always bring the topic around to your skills and qualifications.

THE STRESS INTERVIEW

There are variations to the stress interview, but the basic premise is to test how a person functions under pressure. Can you keep your cool under difficult circumstances? This type of interview is usually conducted by an expert who is well aware of the level of discomfort being created. They are trying to knock you off your stride and raise a reaction – get down to the real "you."

Once in the interview, a less-than-subtle stress tactic is to place the interviewee in an uncomfortable position such as on a wobbly chair. You may be met with icy silence – either right at the beginning of the interview or somewhere in the midst. Who breaks down first? Your tactic should be simply to sit and use the time to observe.

Don't stare at the interviewer. Keep a relaxed demeanor. You will be able to say to yourself, *Ha! this is a stress interview tactic to test my response.*

Occasionally the interviewer will try to fluster the interviewee by barking out an abrasive, challenging question: "So, what makes you think you've got what it takes for this job?" Smile and slide right into your sales pitch. Don't take offense.

AND THE APPLICATION FORM

An often-overlooked but extremely important step in the job-interview process is filling out an application form. Employers report that they are frequently amazed to see the condition of the application form – essential sections not filled in, dates not corresponding to information on the attached résumé, names spelled incorrectly, mistakes scratched out, data put in the wrong place. Check to see if it is a two-sided questionnaire. If you can't fill out the application form accurately and neatly, what does that indicate about your work habits and capabilities? So take the time and treat the application form with due respect. Don't take yourself out of the running by handing in a sloppy or incomplete application form that goes automatically into the reject pile.

CHAPTER SIX

Interviews:
The good, the bad
and the ugly

THE GOOD

Close your eyes. You are about to experience a great job interview. The meeting begins right on time. You are greeted and offered a warm handshake by your interviewer. You are ushered into a quiet private office and shown where you are to sit. There will no interruptions during the meeting. The phone has been put on hold. You are being treated with respect. For the first five minutes, the person is clearly establishing rapport and allowing you to settle down and relax by asking general open-ended questions. You have remembered to sit in a relaxed, non-fidgety way and you feel that you are calm and in control. It is obvious that the interviewer is experienced and businesslike, but at the same time pleasant. Once the interviewer get downs to the actual interview, you recognize that you are being asked behavior-based questions directly related to your work skills. Your tip-off is being asked a "Tell me about a time ...?" question so you can relate a story about how you handled a situation.

During the session, you are allowed to make your sales pitch and describe your skills and accomplishments. You are listened to. As well, you receive essential information about the position – a job description, expectations about overtime, weekend work and travel requirements, salary range, benefits (if it's a full-time permanent position) and opportunities for advancement and personal growth. You are given the chance to ask questions to fully understand the expectations of the employer. As the interview winds up, the next steps in the hiring procedure are carefully explained to you. You are given additional materials to read at home. It is clear that you are being seriously considered for the position.

The interviewer finishes the session on time and asks if you have any further questions. You shake hands again, leave your business card and a fresh résumé, and exchange thanks. The interview is over. It was a pleasant and informative experience. You know that because you have been interviewed by a professional, you have been able to present yourself well. Now open your eyes. But keep that picture in your mind.

 Veteran job-seekers: be prepared for the possibility that your interviewer may be considerably younger than you. Be aware of how you relate to younger colleagues. Are you natural or do you tend to become avuncular/ motherly, intimidating or unintentionally condescending?

THE BAD

We certainly won't visualize a bad interview. No one needs negative thoughts implanted. However, it helps to develop some coping tools to deal with the interview-from-hell.

Bad interviewers are those who, through inexperience, belligerence or sheer stupidity, ask irrelevant, abrupt, inappropriate or blatantly illegal questions. What are illegal questions? These vary from country to country, state to state, province to province. Check both local and federal legislation dealing with unlawful employment practices. Generally speaking, it's illegal to ask questions about race, religion, marital status, sexual orientation, number of children, age, disabilities and health.

The Canadian Human Rights Commission has published *A Guide to Screening and Selection in Employment*. It outlines what can and cannot be asked in an interview. For example, you cannot be asked about your marital status. However, if transfer or travel is part of the job, you can be asked if it will be a difficulty. You cannot be asked about religious affiliation or frequency of church attendance. You can be queried about your ability to fulfill the work schedule requirements. You cannot be asked about health problems such as addiction to alcohol or drugs, hospitalization for emotional reasons or disabilities. But it is considered fair to ask if you have any conditions that might affect your ability to do the job. In the case of disability, it is only permissible to ask questions related to the applicant's ability to perform essential duties of the job and an employer *can* ask about the nature of any accommodation that may be required. For example, will it be necessary for the premises to be wheelchair-accessible?

There are several issues that cannot be discussed in the actual interview, but become admissible after you have been selected. For example, you could be required to take a medical exam if your physical condition is related to job duties. The same holds true for height and weight requirements. After being offered a position, it is valid to ask for a visa or other documentation to confirm that you are legally entitled to work in the country. But none of this should come up in the job interview.

There is a fine line between illegal and just plain rude, inappropriate questions. Inappropriate questions fall within the letter of the law, but are invasive or offensive, for example:

* Do you have a girlfriend?
* Do you live with someone?
* Is that an Italian name?
* Does your spouse work?

Sometimes a less-experienced interviewer does not realize that he is overstepping boundaries. Most larger organizations with a professional human resources department are acutely aware of the laws regulating the permissible questions. However, they also know ways of ferreting out information by clever wording.

Regardless of whether a question is strictly illegal or merely inappropriate, you need a strategy to deal with the situation. It's only human nature to be offended and angry when asked intrusive questions. No one is immune to blatantly discriminatory inquisitions. These occur with women, older employees, people of color or different nationalities, entry-level and student applicants more than other candidates, but no one can fully escape these awkward moments.

So, how to handle inappropriate or illegal questions? If you become confrontational (which is the great temptation), you just alienate the interviewer. Does that mean you should put up with this type of question? No. But you can defuse it by answering in a non-threatening way. Just think of how politicians deflect difficult questions by twisting the answer to suit their own agenda. You always want to put the focus back on your skills and abilities.

If you are more sensitive than the interviewer about admissible questions, you can gently guide them out of a sticky situation. For example, if you are asked:

- **How old are you?** "Well I have more than 20 years of experience in this field and I keep up-to-speed by taking computer courses at my own expense. I think you will find me flexible and adaptable."
- **What religion do you practice?** "I do attend church/synagogue/mosque but I make it a policy never to discuss my personal spiritual beliefs in the workplace. I find it wonderful that there is such a broad scope of belief systems living in harmony in this country.
- **Have you ever received psychiatric treatment or been hospitalized for emotional problems?** "I have no health problems that would stop me from giving my full attention to my job. I exercise at the Y three times a week as my way of relieving any stress I'm experiencing. I find it really works for me."

If the questions become too persistent or offensive, you may have to resort to asking what is the relevance of that question to the job itself. It may cause a bully-interviewer to back off.

It is up to each individual to decide if a complaint should be filed over illegal questions. Such questions may well give you reason to ponder whether or not you are even interested in working for such an organization.

THE UGLY

These are inevitably questions or situations that make you acutely uncomfortable. It may be that poison question you were dreading or the deliberate tactic of the stress interview discussed in the previous chapter. Ugly issues involve questions you really don't want to hear, such as:

- **Have you ever been fired?**

  Ouch, the dreaded question. A simple "no" if that's the case, but you have to provide an honest, direct "yes" if you have been let go with just cause. Be prepared to give the best possible answer to this difficult question. Accept responsibility. Never blame others or criticize. Be brief and to the point. Explain what you learned from the experience.

  Being a victim of downsizing in which you were terminated without due warning is not a case of being fired. It is a case of 1990s workplace reality and most people are sympathetic to someone who has been downsized.

- **Why have you been out of work for several months?**

  This question can seem insensitive and self-evident in times of high unemployment. Again, never whine and blame the general state of the world for your jobless plight. If you are an entry-level candidate, you can explain how looking for that first big break is your job right now. You can discuss the diligent, proactive approach you have been taking to your job search. If you are working part-time, you can explain that you are not out of work, but are looking for satisfying full-time work suitable to your skills and qualifications.

  If you are a more mature candidate, you can emphasize other positive activities you have been engaged in during the months of job searching. Did you take courses to upgrade skills? Were you doing volunteer work? You can point out that you have been searching very actively for the right job and therefore have not just grabbed at the first position offered. You are being selective and certainly you are not desperate. If you were given a good severance package, explain how this has given you the economic security to take time and re-evaluate your career goals.

- **Why haven't you been employed outside of the home for years?**

  Nowadays, this situation pertains to both stay-at-home moms

and dads. However, it is still more of an issue for women who have been out of the work force while their children are young. Preparing a functional-style résumé emphasizing transferable and upgraded skills will sometimes deflect this question. But what to say if you are asked about a lengthy gap in your career? Again, it is a personal response. You might say that you have waited until your children are independent and now you can devote your full attention to your employer. You might discuss the personal re-education and training you took while waiting for your kids to grow up. You might subtly point out how much more dependable a more mature employee will frequently be.

- **Your résumé indicates that you are somewhat of a job-hopper. Why have you had so many jobs?**

  All employers are leery of going to the effort and expense of hiring people who may not stay. In your answer, redirect the emphasis to the present and explain that you are now more focused and goal oriented. Younger people can be forgiven for making a few false-starts in their career. Don't be overly defensive. You can always emphasis that all work experience is broadening. If you have been involved in contract work, explain that you are simply a successful self-employed worker smoothly moving from project to project. Rely on your attitude and interest in the job-at-hand to overcome some of the problems obvious from your résumé.

You are likely to encounter elements of the good, the bad and the ugly in job interviews. Anticipate the good in your interview, but be prepared to handle the bad and the ugly.

Veteran job-seekers: Lifetime learning applies to people of all ages. Taking a course to learn the latest management strategies or upgrading computer skills often has benefits beyond the course itself. There are opportunities to get job leads through fellow classmates and instructors.

CHAPTER SEVEN

Frequently asked questions

Although you can't anticipate all the questions you will be asked in an interview, you can be prepared for general types of questions. Remember: there are no correct answers. There are only smart, positive answers that show you in the best possible light. However, there are *wrong* answers – those that show a lack of commitment and enthusiasm for the position, that prove you don't know the employer's needs, answers that demonstrate you are more interested in "What's in it for me" than what you have to offer to the company.

The basics for handling questions:

- If you don't have an immediate response to a question, take the time to formulate an answer. If you don't understand the question, ask for clarification.
- Keep your reply to two minutes or less. Some interviewees tend to ramble on and repeat themselves. That's why a rehearsal is so important.
- Don't show your despair if you sense the interview isn't going well. This is a performance and you have to stay positive and enthusiastic until the end. You can vent your frustration after you leave the premises. Give a good yell in the privacy of your car.

Here is a sample of the types of questions you are likely to encounter and some suggestions for how to handle them. Keep your answers to the point and aim for about two minutes. Always check to make sure you have the attention of the interviewer.

- **Tell me about yourself.**

This is a stunner of a question if you are not prepared. It's so deceptively simple. But it is probably the most loaded question in the interviewer's arsenal. You might begin by asking the interviewer to narrow down the question. "What are you most interested in knowing about? My prior experiences, accomplishments or skills and training?" Remember, the question isn't about YOU. It is about what you can do for the company.

Begin with the dynamite profile statement you developed for your résumé: "I'm the kind of person who is very detail-oriented, persistent and persuasive. As a television researcher, my persistence paid off in locating and securing the permission to interview a very elusive novelist that gave our program a major scoop. Our audience rating on the night the interview was aired was a record for that kind of literary program. I feel I can bring those same skills and tenacity to this job as well."

Don't ramble on. Use stories to illustrate points you are making. Check to make sure you are on the right track. Ask, "Is this the type of information you are interested in?" This also brings the interviewer back into the conversation and stops you from delivering a soliloquy.

Remember:

Keep it tight and bright – around the two minute mark.

- **What can you do for our company right now?**

In the new work place, employers are looking for experienced people who can step in and, with minimal training, get on with the job. This is often referred to as "just-in-time employment." Here is where doing your research really pays off. If you don't know the details and expectations of the job you are interviewing for, you will bomb with this question. But if you have a clear picture of exactly what the client/employer needs, you can describe the process and timeline, as you foresee it, to get the job done.

In applying for a fundraising position, you could say something like, "I know that you have an urgent need to launch a fundraising capital campaign. I'm very familiar with the fundraising software program you are using. I can start immediately to up-date and greatly expand your direct mail database. I have been involved in two capital campaigns with good results in each."

The only serious caution here is to avoid acting like a know-it-all. No one applying for a job knows all the ins-and-outs of a business or organization. You can put forward your best guess of what the employer needs and you can offer; but don't ever put yourself in the position of *telling* the interviewer what he or she wants. The sin of *hubris* caused endless problems for the ancient Greeks and will not be good for you in a modern-day job interview.

- **What are your strong points?**

People often find it excruciatingly difficult to talk about themselves in a positive way. They think it sounds like boasting. However the interviewer is attempting to assess your sense of self-worth and confidence. This is the time to talk about some of the accomplishments or achievements that you came up with for your résumé, for example:

"I have strong analytical and problem-solving skills. In my last job, I initiated a study and recommended a strategy to streamline the sales force which resulted in a $200,000 per annum saving." Choose three to five strengths and have stories to back them up. Make sure you choose strengths that relate to the position in question.

- **What are your weak points?**

Needless to say, you won't get far by blurting out a litany of your character flaws: "I have a problem getting into the office in the mornings, I never get my expenses in on time, I'm not much of a team player." This may be disarmingly honest, but not very smart.

On the other hand, claiming to have no weaknesses is even less smart. Both you and the interviewer understand that there is a hidden agenda behind this question. How do you deal with self-criticism? How self-aware are you? How do you overcome your own perceived weaknesses? The best answer includes an example of a prior school or work experience in which you recognized a weakness and then overcame it. Never blame others for your weaknesses. Career counselors cite the 5/55 rule: take five seconds to admit a weakness and the other 55 seconds to accent your positive strengths.

- **What are your long-range goals? or Where do you see yourself five years from now?**

You can start by wryly acknowledging that, since the employment world is changing so rapidly, it is hard to predict where anyone will be in terms of career in five years. However, you know that lifelong learning is the key to a successful career and you always have your eye out for workshops and courses to keep you constantly up-to-speed. Briefly outline your long-term goals. Make sure they sound realistic. And never make it sound as if your goal is the interviewer's job.

- **What can you do for us that someone else can't?**

This is not the moment to be self-effacing and say that you are sure there are many people qualified for the position. Like it or not, this is another opportunity for your sales pitch. Now is the time to outline enthusiastically at least three reasons why you are the best candidate. But before answering this question, make sure you fully understand the precise qualifications for the job in question. These are the skills to emphasize in your response.

- **What do you know about our organization?**

Here's an opportunity to demonstrate that you have done your homework. A job applicant for a national book promotion center was asked: "Whom do we primarily represent? The authors or the publishers?" The applicant didn't know. Not very impressive. In your answer, you should go beyond the company itself to place it in context with other competitors in the industry. You can discuss the challenges facing the organization. While you are not expected to have all the answers, you are expected to have a realistic picture of the company's mission and the challenges it faces.

Avoid being the instant expert.
Don't lecture the interviewer about the company's weaknesses or how you - alone - would fix everything.

- **Why do you want to work here?**

Again, research is key to answering this question well. It is important to know exactly what the organization does or the products or services it provides. Praise the company for it's unique characteristics. It is not enough to say, "Well, I want to work in the hospitality industry and you are pretty close to where I am living." Your answer must have valid reasons. "Well, I want to work in the hospitality industry and, in particular, in hotel management. I know that XYZ chain of hotels is world-renowned for its excellent service. I want to learn from the best."

Of course, your answer must sound genuine. You should see any job for which you apply as an opportunity to grow and further your career objectives. If you have no real desire to work for that particular company, perhaps you should re-consider your application. Would it be a beneficial experience for either you or the employer? If not, save the résumé paper, the interview stress and the general irritation - and look harder for a job that suits you.

- **Do you prefer to work alone or as a team player?**

Here the "appropriate " answer depends on the nature of the job. But you must be honest to yourself. If you are a confirmed loner, why bother to apply for a position that requires constant team work and consensus. Employers today are looking for workers who exercise "give and take" to achieve group results, respect others' thoughts and opinions and show leadership qualities. An excellent answer covering all bases is to stress that you enjoy being part of a team working to achieve common goals. Then, at the same time, point out that you are a self-starter and able to finish tasks on your own. Have a few stories ready to illustrate some experiences where you worked effectively in both team and independent situations.

- **Why are you leaving your present job?**

Ouch – if it's because you were let go. (See the discussion in the previous chapter about ways to deal with questions about being fired.) Never bad-mouth the organization where you are presently working. Have a positive spin for your reason for wanting to leave. Give valid reasons such as you find yourself blocked from advancing further and want more of a challenge, or the company is relocating and you don't want to be commuting for well over an hour twice a day. You would rather have more time and energy to actually concentrate on the work itself.

- **You appear to be overqualified for this position. Why are you applying for this particular job?**

This is a dreaded question. Does it mean the interviewer has already made a judgment and written you off? Is it a veiled indication that you are considered too old for the job? Begin with a gentle probe to clarify why the interviewer makes the assumption that you are over-qualified. A woman in her mid-40s applying for a clerical job was asked why someone working on a PhD in Fine Arts would want such a mundane job. She answered that since it was a three-day-a-week job, it would give her the opportunity to combine work and study. She went on to say that the job was in a field she was interested in possibly pursuing. She added that she was extremely reliable, a self-starter and had excellent organizational and written skills. With a grin, she finished by saying she would like to work in such a creative and exciting environment. And she got the job. The over-qualification was no longer an issue.

Your résumé is another way of side-stepping this issue. By using a functional or combination-style résumé, you can omit or compress job experience and leave out dates and job titles. Likewise, you can include only the educational qualifications relevant to the job in question. This may appear deceitful, but you are simply downplaying qualifications that might take you out of the running.

- **Why haven't you found a job?**

There's a maxim: it's easier to find a job when you have a job. The skilfull construction of a functional résumé emphasizing skills and accomplishments may mask the fact that you are currently unemployed. And with today's high level of unemployment and downsizing, there is more sympathy about being out of work. Even a part-time or casual job allows you to answer truthfully that you are employed at the moment. However, if the interviewer knows that you are not presently working, this is a tough question

You may be tempted to answer, "Beats me!" Here's where you have to be upbeat and positive. No whining or moaning about the lousy economy or how the boomers are hogging all the jobs. Simply state that you have the skills and qualifications and are looking forward to a challenging job. If you had retired and are returning to work, you can downplay the retirement aspect by simply saying you took a time-out and used the opportunity to renew. Now you are keen to contribute both your experience and upgraded skills.

- **Describe an especially difficult problem you have had to deal with in a previous job.**

The key here is your problem-solving ability. The interviewer is really asking, "Do you have a system to cope with problems?" This is an excellent opportunity to use the storytelling technique of SITUATION – ACTION – RESULT. What the problem was, what action you took, what the outcome or result was. For example: "Because of our budget limitations, I reviewed our printed materials and realized that we could get by with one generic brochure to fulfill a variety of functions – to send out to prospective students, to include in our fundraising kit and for general publicity. So I analyzed the essential information needed and had a multipurpose brochure designed. We also scaled down the size of the brochure to cut down on postage costs. In all, we saved ourselves about $4,000."

One of the essential skills employers are looking for is the ability to think critically, act logically to evaluate the situation and then be able to solve the problem and make a decision.

- **How do you deal with time management?**

Use examples to describe how you organize your workday. You may have a simple, yet effective system of list making. If you are using a professional time management system, such as one of the software personal organizers, explain how effectively you use it. If you are a recent university graduate, describe how you prioritized course work, assignments and extracurricular activities. Stress that you have a system to juggle several balls in the air at the same time without dropping any of them. Being able to handle multiple tasks and meet deadlines is a priceless asset. Show through specifics that you have this ability.

- **How do you handle stress?**

Who doesn't get stressed these days? People with full-time positions are working harder and longer hours. Those in the temp world doing contract work are juggling multiple tasks while trying to get leads on the next assignment. Here's an opportunity to assure the prospective employer that you have figured out a stressbuster. In today's society it would be suspect to answer that you simply avoid stress. Instead, use the storytelling technique to describe how you have handled pressure or tight deadlines in the past. You can add what you do to get rid of the stress after work hours - smash a ball around the racquet court, jog, swim, yoga - whatever you do to relieve tension (and make sure that you do have a way to get rid of pent-up stress).

- **What was the last book you read/film you saw?**

Why are they asking you this question? Certainly not to be treated to a book or film review. The interviewer is simply trying to find out more about you. Be honest, yet selective in your answer. There's absolutely nothing wrong with reading the latest steamy potboiler or seeing a mindless summer blockbuster, but make sure you also have other examples: in particular, books on personal or employment self-improvement. Never take the risk of saying a title you haven't read - you never know what book is on your interviewer's bedside table.

- **What are your salary expectations?**

Although you are advised to attempt to deflect this answer until a time when you have been offered a job, persistent interviewers often will not let the question drop. It can be a screening-out device to avoid getting to advanced stages in the hiring process and then discovering that the gap between what you expect and what the company is offering is too great. If at all possible, turn the question around and make the interviewer give the figure. "I'd be interested to know what your company pays for positions that require my level of skills and experience." If that doesn't work, you can hedge by saying, "I'm aware of the general range of compensation in the industry for someone with my qualifications, but I'd feel better discussing salary when I have a clearer picture of exactly what the job requires."

- **May we check your references?**

This a simple response if you are confident that you have chosen your references wisely. It is a deadly question if your bluff has been called and you've included names of people you hope will impress the interviewer – people who may not actually have first-hand knowledge about you. Always assume that your references will be checked. Be sure you can comfortably answer, "Yes, please do." Even better, at that point give your interviewer a list with names, titles and company phone numbers of your references.

- **Do you have any questions?**

This is often used as a close by the interviewer, but you should consider it a golden opportunity to leave on a high note. Ask positive questions such as, "What would be my first task?" "Whom would I be reporting to?" or "Is there a job description I could take away with me to study?" This creates the not-so-subtle assumption that you consider yourself to be in the running for the position. Be careful not to ask questions that the interviewer cannot answer. Suddenly you have made her feel uncomfortable. It is definitely not the time to ask about salary, the benefits package and how much vacation time you will be getting. That comes at the next stage when you are negotiating for the job.

Watch out

Anticipate and have answers prepared for questions you would rather avoid. Interviewers always zero right in on our Achilles' heel. However, if you have thought about these issues in advance and have a straightforward, honest, brief answer, you can neatly defuse the difficulty. Some people suggest that you circumvent a sticky situation by bringing it up first. That's a call. While there's no advantage in pointing out a potential problem, if it's unavoidably obvious (e.g., you are seven months pregnant!) confront it. "As you can see, I am about to have a baby but I understand that the position in question is not available right away and I have excellent child-care support in place."

CHAPTER EIGHT

Seven common job interview mistakes

Take the healthy attitude about learning from mistakes. After all, everyone makes them. With time, we can look back and laugh at them. However, at the moment, it can be embarrassing and perhaps even cost you the job. Here are seven common pitfalls to avoid.

1.   Don't Bring Distractions

Interviewers report that some candidates have been known to bring along a friend or relative for moral support. This is *always* a mistake. Imagine the impression it makes if you feel it necessary to come accompanied by Dad or a best friend. An interview is a solitary event; and so is the waiting room. Some employers are observing your behavior even as you sit and wait for your appointment. If you spend your time chatting loudly with a friend or, worse, laughing and showing off, you've kissed the job goodbye before you ever reach the interview itself.

On the other hand, even though applying for a job is a solitary pursuit, don't sit in the waiting area listening to your Walkman. Take the time to look around and observe, to prepare yourself for the interview to come. Likewise, leave the cell phone at home or at least turn it off and tuck it into your briefcase or purse. No one is going to be impressed – and many office people find these devices an annoyance.

2.   First Impressions Count

It's a cardinal rule never to be late for an interview. Always give yourself extra time. Of course, the unexpected can happen –

there's an accident on the highway, you're stuck in traffic, the subway system breaks down, the baby-sitter is late. How can you recover from being late for the interview? If possible, phone as soon as you realize that you will be delayed. Be calm, apologize and briefly explain the problem. Listen carefully to their reaction. They may suggest rescheduling for later in the same day or moving the interview to another day.

If you can not get in contact, upon arrival apologize and explain the cause for your lateness. Make sure that the interviewer is acutely aware that YOU find being late a serious problem. Don't appear to accept lateness as okay. Some interviewers will ask you if you want a few minutes to get yourself ready for the interview. Take them. You'll need the time to calm down, get your smile working and get your brain focused on the interview ahead.

3.   Being Unprepared

Nothing is more damaging than not being able to answer the question, "What do you know about our company?" Your answer should make it clear that you have done some kind of homework. You should give the impression that it is your research knowledge that has given you a desire to be part of the organization. Anyone who still subscribes to the "fly by the seat of your pants" method of job interviewing, is competing with candidates who have gone to the effort to do research.

But what if the worst happens? Then do a quick study. Check out the company magazine in the waiting room, the pictures on the wall, the product displays on the shelves. Ask the receptionist if there is a catalogue or company newsletter you can look at while you're waiting. Don't pretend to be an expert on the basis of 20 minutes of desperate research, but anything you've learned from this might be helpful in the interview.

4.   Don't be a Know-It-All

There is a fine line between being unprepared and appearing too cocky. Don't assume you know as much about the company as the person doing the interview. Listen more than you talk. Although your purpose is to sell your skills, bragging is not an effective method. Likewise, an interviewer is rarely impressed with name dropping.

One job applicant proudly told the interviewer how much he knew about the company objectives and organization based upon some insight he'd been given by a friend a few weeks before the interview. He mentioned the the name of a particular vice president as a woman who was really "going places" with the company goals.

Unfortunately, the vice president had already gone other places, jumping from the company to a competitor just the previous week. This information left the job applicant considerably embarrassed but taught him some of the virtues of humility.

5. Don't Have Foot-in-Mouth Disease

It's difficult to recover when you've rambled on about the inadequacies or obsolescence of the computer system used in your present job only to discover the same system is used in the organization where you are interviewing. Or bad-mouthing a person in the industry only to discover that the interviewer holds him/her in high esteem. Discretion is essential for the job-seeker. Negatives are to be avoided.

When you do stick your foot firmly in your mouth and it's obvious, all you can do is apologize. "Sorry, I didn't understand the whole situation," is a handy phrase for this.

6. At a Loss for Words

Although we all hope it never happens, there may come a moment when our minds simply go blank due to nervousness. If you suddenly find yourself at a loss for words during the interview, stay cool. Take a moment to regain your composure. A short silence is often taken as a pause to consider the question. What seems an eternity to you, may not to the interviewer. Take a deep breath. Ask the interviewer to repeat the question in order to gain time and get back on track. Casually review your résumé or refer to a small cue card on which you've jotted down the main skills you want to emphasize during the interview. If you're prone to freezing up in stressful situations, prepare a strategy. Perhaps it is just a phrase. "I'm sorry, I've lost my train of thought. I'll start my answer again."

7. Don't Leave a Bitter After-Taste

Don't sabotage yourself by lashing out in disappointment after receiving a rejection letter or phone call. You never know how the cards will fall in the long run. You may have been a strong contender for the job and are being kept in mind for the next opening. The successful applicant may turn down the offer or not work out. Continue to be professional.

If you are given the bad news by phone, thank the caller for the courtesy of contacting you in person and considering you for the position. You can express your disappointment in a positive fashion by saying that you were very impressed with the organization and keen to contribute to its continuing success. Emphasis that you would like to stay in touch and be considered for other possible opportunities. If you are contacted by letter, send back a short thank-you note for the opportunity to interview for the position and again ask to be kept in mind. Foster an on-going relationship.

Bitter recriminations only hurt YOU.

One unsuccessful candidate sent along an expense claim for mileage and a meal in a letter expressing his annoyance at the wasted time in coming for the interview. Needless to say, his travel expense was rejected and he took himself out of the running for future consideration. As difficult as it is to do, don't take an unsuccessful job interview as a personal rejection.

CHAPTER NINE

Students and recent graduates

After years of being in school, you are finally faced with the career world. Understandably you may have self-doubts. "I've never done this work before." "I will need direction and training." "I'm not sure how to act in business meetings." As you go into job interviews, check off in your mind all the positive attributes you offer an employer as a newcomer:

- energy and fresh ideas
- flexibility
- state-of-the-art skills
- eagerness to prove yourself
- lower wage demands

Surveys have shown that the highest-priority sets of skills being sought by Canadian employers are **computer, communication** and **interpersonal skills**. For work in any office environment, employees are expected to have basic word processing, spreadsheet and database management skills along with the ability to handle E-mail, send and receive files and navigate the Internet or an external Bulletin Board system (BBS). Even if not entering a technical line of work, job-seekers should know how to operate a calculator and handle basic arithmetic. While older workers may have trouble with some of these skills, recent graduates are likely to be much more at home in the computer world. You may take these skills for granted, it is very important to stress them both in your résumé and during the job interview.

A founder of one of Canada's leading-edge digital media communications companies expressed his frustration at his employees – even the younger ones – reluctance to take responsibility and be self-directed. It seems the old hierarchical system with bosses telling workers what to do is a difficult concept to shake. Employers are looking for people with good people skills who can work either independently or handle the "give and take" of group dynamics. As a new graduate, you've mastered considerably more flexibility than most older job applicants.

Recruiters sometimes complain that recent graduates frequently emphasis their educational qualifications and not real-life experiences. And while that is understandable, it is more effective to shift the focus to demonstrate how you can apply your learning to the job at hand. Another mistake newcomers make is apologizing for a lack of work-related experience. If you are interviewing for an entry-level position, the interviewer should be well aware of and sympathetic to the fact that you just starting out.

First-time job seekers

If you are looking for your first job and have no direct work experience, don't despair. Talk about extracurricular activities to demonstrate skills which can be transferred to a job situation. For example, have you been on a sports team? You can describe your dedication to the sport – getting up at 5:30 a.m. every school morning in order to train with the synchronized swim team. You can further stress that working as part of a team is an essential ingredient for success in synchronized swimming. Have you done any baby-sitting? You can use satisfied clients as references to vouch for your maturity and sense of responsibility.

THE QUESTIONS YOU'LL FACE

Here are ten questions students and graduates are often asked. The sample answers are simply guidelines. Be sure to prepare your own unique responses to such questions.

- **Why did you chose the university you attended?**

There are some universities with more prestige than others and its assumed that their graduates have the upper hand in the job market. But it's not necessarily so. Employers are interested in your motive for choosing a university. It has to be more than its name or family tradition. However, there are some courses where graduates are virtually assured of instant employment. For example graduates from the School of Animation and Design at Sheridan College, in Ontario are immediately snapped up by the international entertainment industry. Explain the rationale for your choice. "I researched all the journalism courses offered across Canada and decided that Ryerson's School of Journalism offered the best opportunities for my choice of specialization in magazine writing."

- **What courses/subjects did you like best or least?**

Clearly, courses which directly relate to the job in question should be emphasized. For example, a recent graduate in Fashion Marketing applying for an entry-level position in management might respond. "Although I loved the History of Costume course, one of the most useful courses for me was Fashion Retail Buying where I learned to use state-of-the-art business application software to deal effectively with merchandise management problems."

- **How has your education prepared you for this job?**

If you have a specialized degree in the field where you are applying for a position, this is an easier question to answer. If you have a general high school diploma or liberal arts degree, you can discuss transferable employability skills such as the ability to think critically, problem solve and manage time. Stress computer skills and knowledge of other languages. Many students go on after a university degree to get a more job-focused community college diploma. Some universities are offering combined programs to blend the theoretical knowledge from university with the practical know-how from a community college.

The best answer always draws on a detail from something you did in school and relates it to the job for which you are applying. "In studying urban geography, we did a number of surveys and I learned to be quite comfortable doing survey work at malls and over the phone. This has given me the kind of background that would be useful to your company in doing telephone canvassing." Obviously the detail and the application will change from job to job.

- **How did you finance your education?**

If you used student loans supplemented with part-time work, briefly explain how you managed your time and expenses. Perhaps you combined work with part-time courses. If you had to take a time-out during your education in order to earn tuition money, talk about that. This shows your tenacity and dedication to gaining an education.

Avoid answering that your parents paid for the whole shot including all spending money. As lucky as you might have been, it does not impress employers about your initiative and independence. Even if you have never had a part-time job, surely there is some volunteer or co-op job related experience you can emphasize.

- **What summer jobs have you had?**

There is more than one motive behind this question. The interviewer is probing to find out more about your attitudes and maturity. If you have never worked during vacations, why not? Valid reasons include fast-tracking by taking summer school courses or travelling to improve language skills. However, if you were loafing around at the family summer cottage during vacations, this will not be impressive.

A further question may be asked about how you went about getting a summer job. The answer should illustrate your initiative and perseverance. No matter how menial the jobs have been, you have experience in being an employee. Stress that these summer jobs taught you about responsibility, the value of money, time management and getting along with other employees and customers.

- **What Leadership Roles Have You Held?**

If you are just beginning your adult work life, you are unlikely to have examples of professional leadership roles. But leadership takes many forms. For example, those reports from camp counselors which made your parents gloat with pride have a greater use. They can be used as verifiable recommendations of leadership, "As the cabin's most experienced member, Daniel assumed a very influential leadership position. ... On our five-day canoe trip down the historic French River, Daniel was instrumental in maintaining enthusiasm and took a responsible role in helping out the less-experienced campers." Review all school report cards, appraisals from volunteer or co-op work to remind yourself of situations in which you demonstrated a strong leadership role. Prepare and rehearse a couple of stories to describe times when you were a leader at school, summer camp, or in a part-time job situation.

- **Have you been involved in any volunteer work?**

Today's employers are keen to hear about volunteer experience from prospective employees. Many non-profit agencies give their volunteers excellent training courses and opportunities to take on responsible tasks. Volunteering helps you build up a reference list. Occasionally volunteer jobs become permanent employment.

Again, you should tie your volunteer experience into the skills it developed, or show how it relates to the job at hand. "Working for the Red Cross in disaster relief taught me a great deal about teamwork ... and long hours. When the river is about to come over the sandbags, there's no time for arguments or coffee breaks."

- **What do you do in your spare time?**

If you are a couch potato or addict of computer games, don't volunteer that information. Chose interests and hobbies somewhat related to the job. If you participate in a sport, briefly describe your pleasure in being with other people and getting much needed exercise. This illustrates your teamwork abilities and healthy way to deal with stress.

Before getting your first job, you have some paperwork to do. You will need a Social Insurance Number (SIN) Card. Forms are available at a your local Human Resource Center office. The completed application must be accompanied by a Canadian provincial birth certificate (or Canadian Immigration Record and Visa of Record of Landing, unexpired immigration form or Refugee Status Claim). If your application is in order, it takes approximately three weeks to receive a SIN card. If you don't already have one, it's time to open up a bank account. Many employers prefer to pay by direct-deposit to the employee's bank account.

- **Are you looking for a permanent or temporary job?**

Once burned, twice shy. Employers do not appreciate going to the time and effort of training staff to have them leave within a few months to return to school or to go off around the world. You are unlikely to get a good reference from a company who took you on in good faith if you leave within a short time. And you could make it difficult for other young job-seekers.

In answering, you should reassure the interviewer that you have finished your formal education and are now ready to gain some solid work experience. You should emphasize the commitment that you do anticipate – two years, five years, moving up in the company, whatever. And you might want to ask them the same question. Is this a full-time position with the opportunity for advancement? Ask about the company's training and promotion policy. This gives the interviewer a sense that you'll be around for the long haul.

- **Would you take further training if it was required for the job?**

An enthusiastic yes is the right answer. For example, some financial institutions will reimburse new recruits if they successfully take the Canadian Securities Course. (This is a highly recognized investment course for anyone who plans to work in the financial service industry. It is a self-study course with optional seminars held in major Canadian cities.) At a later stage in the job negotiation process, you can ask who is responsible for course fees, would the training take place during work hours or on your own time during evenings or weekends and does your job security depend on a successful outcome?

Always keep in mind the objective behind these questions. You are one of many graduates with similar qualifications. What can give you the edge? Knowing what employers need. They are looking for young people who are creative, responsible and can think critically both independently and in team situations. They want to know what you can do for them. Give them lots of reasons for hiring YOU.

Here are a few extremely helpful Web sites to visit. Bear in mind that the information on the Net rapidly changes and URLs (Universal Resource Locator) can change.

YOUTH RESOURCE NETWORK OF CANADA
www.youth.gc.ca
This site helps young people bridge the gap between school and the labor market. It provides quick links to many other useful sites. Check out the virtual interview sites which provide multiply choice options to a variety of possible interview questions.

CANADA WORK INFONET
www.workinfone.ca/
It serves as an internet directory (like a telephone book) providing up to 1300 links ranging from career development, financial help and community services across Canada.

WORKSEARCH
www.worksearch.gc.ca
This site has been designed to help job seekers through all aspects of the work search process. It includes help on preparing a résumé and tips on interview skills.

CHAPTER TEN

Tests

Many employers will ask job candidates to take some type of test or analysis as part of the hiring procedure. There are many tests to fulfill various functions. Regardless of the type, you have to make the decision of whether or not you agree to being tested. A refusal usually means that you have taken yourself out of contention for the job.

In gentler times, people in financial industries may have expected to take a skills tests to demonstrate their mathematical abilities. Secretarial personnel would take typing and shorthand tests to prove their words per minute. Today there are a variety of tests to find out more about a potential employee's personality, teamwork and leadership qualities, skills and intelligence.

SKILLS TESTING

If you reach the stage where you are seriously being considered for the position, you may be asked to take tests to confirm the claims made in your résumé. For example, a competition for an executive assistant position had a series of practical tasks for candidates to demonstrate their proficiency in job-related skills. First the applicants were given a memorandum to test for spelling and grammatical ability, attention to detail and the ability to quickly grasp essential facts. The candidates were given 15 minutes to review the document, identity typos and grammatical errors and absorb the salient facts. Later on they were asked to give a verbal summary of the memorandum.

Here's a similar test: can you catch the typos and grammatical errors in the following sample paragraph?

Before beginning that discussion, Bill indicated that the ministrys financial targets for the coming year our not know and will not be known until late Febuary at the earliest. Even when the Ministry tragets are know, how each agency will be effected will depend on the Ministry's core service restucturing strategy which is under developed but be no means complete.

Next the candidates were invited to view a videotaped management meeting and take minutes. Accurate minute taking was an important element for the executive assistant position. Finally they were asked to listen to Dictaphone instructions to produce a letter. Certain details such as the name of a government official and a simple percentage calculation were left to the resourcefulness of the candidate. (Only one person found the correct name of the government official by using a government directory.) This type of arduous testing separates the truly qualified from the pretenders.

Be wary if an employer asks you to work without salary for a period of time in order to prove your abilities. Often younger people fall prey to this request. Occasionally candidates are asked to prepare sample materials (such as a press release) or develop a project concept, marketing or business plan. (Some professionals such as architects or artists can expect juried competitions in which detailed designs must be submitted for consideration.) Where does the prospective employee draw the line? How many hours of "free" work are reasonable? Who owns the copyright on the material? These delicate issues need to be addressed. Try to get the sample work project more clearly defined. How many hours does the employer consider reasonable? Who absorbs the costs for materials? It comes down to asking yourself how far you are prepared to go to demonstrate your abilities. It is worthwhile to do some checking around to make sure that the organization is entirely ethical.

As part of the pre-screening process, you may encounter problem-solving tests similar to GMATs to confirm that your hard skills – verbal and mathematical – are adequate for the job. Remember that today's employers are looking for people who can read and comprehend written materials and understand and solve mathematical problems. Emphasis is put on the ability to think critically and logically to evaluate situations and solve problems.

PERSONALITY TESTS

The soft skills – such as personal management and teamwork – are equally sought after by today's employers. A number of analysis systems have been developed to reveal the candidate's strengths and weaknesses. One such management assessment system is used by over 55,000 organizations in 40 different countries worldwide. Respondents select the words or phrases that most and least describe him or her. This uncovers a person's preferred behavior style. Such an assessment can be further interpreted to offer more specific insights into the person's management, technical, sales or any other number of skills.

Here is a report on a very non-competitive person who was audited for sales skills. "Closing, particularly in relation to new contacts, is likely to be Ms. X's potential weakness. As she is non-antagonistic by nature, she is likely to worry a little about rejection that could occur as a result of pushing for orders. The result, therefore, is that Ms. X may not always face up to the objections of the prospect and may lack the tenacity required in a good sales close. This results from her kind and non-demanding nature. It should be noted that Ms. X has good abilities when dealing with situations which are of a longer-term negotiable nature." The report went on to recommend that the respondent be given training in closing techniques. If a company was looking for a hotshot salesperson to make fast closes, the candidate wouldn't have a chance of being hired. But if the position was for a planned-gift fundraiser to nurture wealthy philanthropists to leave their fortune to a specific charity, Ms. X would be a perfect match of needs and skills.

These assessment tools are not used as the sole criteria for choosing a candidate. However, they are useful to the prospective employer to get a better understanding of what makes you tick.

If you do agree to testing, always find out what type of test it is. Ask if you can get the results and interpretation. If you have test phobia, will that be taken into account and can you retake it? How influential are the test results in the final decision about your suitability? Who is giving the test? Who will be privy to the results of your test? Just the human resources department, your department head, other members of your team?

DRUG TESTING

It's not just world-class athletes who are subjected to drug testing these days. Many of the United States Fortune 500 companies automatically ask prospective employees to agree to drug testing before hiring. Canadians working for United States branch plants may be asked to take a drug test. Canadian truck drivers operating in the United States are subject to widespread drug and alcohol testing. It is The Canadian Human Rights Commission's opinion that mandatory drug testing is considered discriminatory *unless* there is a clear demonstration by the employer that the policy is rationally connected to the performance of the job. People working in high-risk occupations such as police officers, ambulance drivers or pilots may face drug testing as part of the hiring process.

If you do find yourself in a situation where drug testing is requested, be very careful to fully understand the procedure. You must know what over-the-counter medications and other non-drug substances may create a false positive result. Most reputable companies will provide a complete list of substances that may interfere with the results.

To prepare, you should make a list of absolutely everything you have put in mouth in the past few weeks – every painkiller, indigestion remedy, health food supplement – this is serious business since your reputation is at stake.

You should also have a commitment for a follow-up test if, for some horrible reason, the results are false positive.

HANDWRITING SAMPLES

May we have a sample of your handwriting for analysis? Oh please, are you kidding? No, this is an accepted practice for staff selection in many European corporations, especially in France. The use of graphology or graphoanalysis is not widespread in North America, but it is relied on by some companies. Proponents of this testing system maintain that handwriting analysis will reveal a great deal of essential information about the person such as mental abilities, attitudes, traits and self-concept. Some less-than-scrupulous companies may have your handwriting analyzed without your permission. If you are asked to submit a sample (and you are not applying for a position as a calligrapher), you may question why they want this handwriting sample.

CHAPTER ELEVEN

Follow-up

Immediately after the interview – when your impressions are the most accurate – debrief yourself by making notes. If you didn't get business cards from your interviewers, jot down the names and correct titles of all the people you met. Did you promise to send any follow-up materials? Write it down.

Review your own performance in the interview. Did you emphasis your skills that relate directly to the job in question. How was your body language and voice? Did you remember to smile occasionally and make eye contact with the interviewer? Did you actually ask for the job at the end of the interview? An honest self-evaluation helps you to improve your job-interviewing technique.

Then take time to quietly reflect and evaluate your interview and the potential job opportunity. Bottom line – now that you hopefully have a clearer picture, do you still want the job? Ask yourself these questions:

- What did I learn about the position?
- Does it match with my short-/long-term career goals?
- What opportunities for learning/advancement does it offer?
- Do I feel I can handle the work/the level of responsibility?
- Is it challenging enough?
- Did the atmosphere make me comfortable? Can I work with those people?
- Were the demands suitable to my personal situation – travel, overtime, weekend work?

Notify your reference people that you had the interview and

that they might expect a phone call. Give them the name of the person who may be making the call. Describe the interview and the skills you emphasized.

CHOOSING YOUR REFERENCES

A rogue reference can sabotage your chances. You may have done a great interview, the employer is keen and takes that next step of phoning to confirm his positive impression. If your reference person is over-effusive, hesitant, or – worse still – negative, alarm bells will start to ring. The prospective employer may have second thoughts or move on to another candidate.

So how do you choose your references? Carefully! It's easier if you have a job history and can use previous bosses and colleagues who can speak positively about your work performance. It is best to have a range of references from a supervisor or manager to a co-worker and perhaps to someone under your management. That covers all bases in getting the full picture of your work and management style. If you are an entry-level candidate, select people who can talk about your educational and extracurricular achievements – teachers, camp directors, supervisors of any volunteer work you did, sports coaches, bosses of part-time and summer jobs – who can vouch for your leadership, initiative, integrity, teamwork skills, work or study habits.

- Never give out a name as a reference without checking for permission first.
- Provide references with a copy of your résumé.
- Discuss with them the points you would like them to emphasis and check to confirm that they are in agreement.
- Have a number of references so one person is not burdened by too many phone calls.

Nurture your reference people throughout your job search process. If it is convenient, arrange to meet with them and go over the strengths and accomplishments you want them to promote with the inquiring employer. Keep in touch with them regularly throughout your quest for work. Inform them of your progress and, in particular, let them know the outcome of any reference check.

These are the types of questions prospective employers may ask your references. Will the people you have chosen be able to give positive answers?

- What are his (her) strengths and weaknesses based on your experience?
- Is he (she) a team player? What about leadership qualities?
- Is he (she) well organized?
- How responsible is he (she)? What about attendance, making deadlines, fulfilling commitments?
- What were his (her) main duties and responsibilities in your organization?
- Do you think he (she) could perform the duties of this position?

If you don't want your current employer to know that you are actively searching for another job, a reference from an immediate boss can be tricky. The best policy is to be honest and negotiate for that particular reference to be checked after you have a firm offer. However, if you have included the name of your current employer on your résumé, there is nothing to prevent the interviewer from making a phone call without your permission.

No matter how you felt the interview went, within 24 hours send a follow-up letter addressed personally to the person (or persons) you met. As always, be sure to check the spelling of all names. Begin by thanking them for the chance to interview for the position. Here is the opportunity to add any pertinent information about your unique qualifications for the position. It also gives you the opportunity to clarify questions you might have fumbled over. End the letter by stating that you will be in contact by phone within a specified time period. You have given yourself the opening for another contact. Keep it brief – no more than a page. Although most people make it a formal business letter, others use a handwritten note, to be more distinctive. To some extent, it is a matter of the corporate culture.

Make good on your promise with a phone call. It shows that you follow through on your commitments. It may be very difficult to actually talk to your interviewer. Voice mail has become an effective way of screening out calls. Modern wisdom suggests that people can sometimes be directly reached by either phoning shortly before the beginning of the work day or slightly after the office closing time. Of course, call display is an effective way of screening out unwanted phone calls. You may decide to leave a message in voice mail. It's yet another of those many judgement calls, since frequent messages can be very annoying. On the other hand, one call a week may be taken as a sign of persistence and confidence.

Remember, if often takes weeks for companies to go through the hiring process. Just because you haven't heard doesn't necessarily mean that you are out of the running.

NEGOTIATING FOR THE JOB

Congratulations! The job has been offered to you. What do you do now? Stay cool. Act professionally. A career coach has coined the expression "right jobs" and "right now jobs." Is this a job that will advance your career goals? Or is it a holding-pattern job? Can you afford to turn it down and continue on with your search? Or is it an opportunity to keep your head above water as you persist in your job search? Will the work allow you to develop or exercise skills that are transferable to other jobs? Perhaps the salary is below your expectations, but the training opportunities will eventually make you much more marketable. Only you can realistically evaluate the benefits of the offered job.

You may get a formal letter outlining salary and benefits being offered. Or, you may be invited to another interview to discuss the offer. Before this interview, sit down and make a complete list of what you need to receive in the job offer. You will be more respected if you negotiate the best package rather than just accept whatever's offered. Negotiation must be done with skilful assertion, not pushy aggression. It's a business deal. Show that you value yourself and the skills you are bringing to the company.

Here's a partial list of negotiable items. Add your own unique requirements. Decide in advance what's essential and what's dispensable.

Financial

> base salary
> salary review
> signing bonus
> commission
> bonuses
> stock options/profit sharing
> cost-of-living allowance
> severance package

Benefits

> vacation time
> flextime
> overtime or lieu time
> paid sick leave
> medical/dental plan
> life/disability insurance
> pension
> tuition/training

Value-Added Perks

> company car
> cellular phone
> car insurance
> mileage and maintenance allowance
> expenses
> parking
> computer

professional association memberships
fitness club membership
subscriptions to professional periodicals
clothing allowance
relocation expenses

Needless to say, be realistic about your expectations. In today's world of contract work, many of these benefits are no longer in the picture. And it certainly depends on your seniority and qualifications. While it may be appropriate for an on-camera television interviewer to ask about a clothing allowance, it would be highly inappropriate for an entry-level receptionist. It would be essential for someone who is expected to use their personal car for company business to nail down a mileage and auto maintenance agreement. Discussing a severance package is somewhat similar to talking about a prenuptial agreement. It may seem dispassionate, but you will be extremely thankful later on.

Once you have agreed to a package, make sure you get it in writing. It is usual for the letter of agreement to come from the employer. However, if it is not forthcoming (and you may want to ask why) you can write the letter yourself and have it signed by both parties. Never rely on a verbal commitment.

At this point, you might be saying: a permanent full-time job with full benefits package – dream on. The reality is that more and more jobs are contract positions. However, you may be able to arrange for some of the items outlined as possible benefits.

SALARY NEGOTIATION

This can be the trickiest part of the bargaining procedure. Try to avoid questions of salary until you have a firm job offer. Martin Yate in *"Knock 'em Dead"* recommends that you establish three figures: a minimum, a realistic midpoint, and a dream salary. The *minimum* (for your benefit alone) is your absolute basic cash requirement in order to survive. The realistic is based on solid research to find out what your skills are worth in the current market. Yate describes the dream salary as "the figure that would make you smile, drop dead and go to heaven on the spot." In today's employment environment, it is probably just as wise to keep the dream salary to yourself and concentrate on the middle ground. But it is much easier to negotiate down than up. Therefore don't lowball if asked for an expected salary.

Often employers will try to put the ball back in your court by asking you what is your current salary. You can try to deflect the question by suggesting that the two jobs are very different and thus not a valid comparison. If you are considerably underpaid, you can add to the base salary the dollar value for all your benefits.

NO DEAL

People have a difficult time turning down a job. We feel panicky. What if I don't get another offer? But there's no point in taking a position in which you feel exploited or unhappy. If you simply cannot come to an acceptable agreement about the terms, graciously reject the offer while reinforcing your appreciation for the opportunity to interview for the position. Never burn your bridges. In a long career you often find yourself across the negotiating table again with some of the same people. Follow up with a courteous letter thanking the company for the offer, while politely declining.

Negotiating is not an innate ability – it is a learned skill. Nearly everyone is fearful of being rejected and so finds it hard to ask. However, the more you practice negotiating the easier it becomes. Key points to remember in negotiating:

- Know what you want.
- Ask for what you want.
- Stay open-minded and flexible.
- Go for win-win (both parties feel they got what they wanted).
- Stay objective and detached. Don't get emotional.

CHAPTER TWELVE

What! I didn't get the job?

You may think it counterproductive to include a chapter on possible rejection in a book on doing a great interview. But it does happen sometimes - the interview goes very well - yet you still don't get the offer. The point is to make even this a positive opportunity.

No one said that life is fair. The job decision has been a draw between yourself and another candidate. The final choice may have been very rational or the result of flipping a coin. The successful candidate may have had the edge by knowing someone in the organization. Whatever the reason, you are faced with rejection - and no one finds that easy to handle. However, the attitude you adopt to this disappointment makes a fundamental difference later on. If you become discouraged and bitter, this will come across in future interviews. If you have the courage and self-confidence to accept defeat and move on, your positive attitude will shine through. Don't take the failure to get the job as a personal rejection.

Consider all interviews as useful: a chance to build up experience and confidence, learn some of the pitfalls, make yourself known in the industry. Although you may not have been offered that particular contract or job, you never know what the future holds. You may have been the runner-up and are being kept in mind for the next project or permanent job opening. The person hired may not work out. The interviewer may move on to another company and need someone with exactly your qualifications.

However, if you are consistently being turned down, it may be time for some honest self-appraisal to try and figure out the problem.

Is there a common pattern? Are you applying for inappropriate jobs - too senior or too junior? Are you being realistic? Do you have all the required skills and work experience? Are you coming across as nervous and lacking confidence? Does your appearance need work? Then come back to the bottom line. Did you have something to offer the company? Or were you just looking for a job?

One way to find out any problem is to simply ask the person who turned you down. But this has to be handled skilfully. People are reluctant to offer criticism and certainly don't want to be put on the defensive or listen to bitter recriminations. And it is often very difficult to reach these busy people. But if you are lucky enough to establish contact, try to get some constructive feedback on what they felt were your shortcomings or lack of qualifications or skills. Make it clear that you want to learn from this experience. Listen very carefully and take notes on what is said. This is not the time to argue or justify that you, in fact, do have that skill. You obviously didn't get that across to them in the interview. Learn from it and know that, in the next situation, you certainly will emphasize all your skills.

Ask the person for any advice they may be able to offer about opportunities with other companies or the names of people to contact. Can they suggest any courses or workshops that would enhance your future prospects?

The YWCA of Metropolitan Toronto has compiled a very useful survey based on data from over 150 personnel officers on the most frequent reasons why people are not hired. They are not arranged in priority but all of them turn off an interviewer:

- Poor personal appearance
- Overaggressive, conceited, "know-it-all attitude"
- Poor voice, diction, grammar, inability to express oneself
- No purpose or goals for vocation
- Lack of interest and enthusiasm
- Lack of confidence and poise
- Too much emphasis on money
- Poor or borderline academic achievement
- Unwillingness to start at bottom; expects too much, too soon

- Makes excuses, reluctant to talk about unfavorable things in his (her) work and academic record
- No job experience
- Lacks knowledge of opportunities in field in which trained
- No interest or knowledge of company or industry
- Poor handling of personal finances
- No interest in community activities
- Inability to take criticism
- Lack of appreciation of the value of experience
- Late to interview without a good reason
- Failure to express thanks for interviewer's time
- Limp or lifeless handshake
- Shows high degree of indecision
- Sloppy or incomplete application form
- Merely "shopping around" for a job
- Wants job for only short time
- Too cynical
- Intolerant, strong prejudices
- Narrow interests
- Failure to ask questions about the job
- High-pressure type
- Lack of tact
- Lack of maturity
- Lack of courtesy
- Critical of former employers
- Name-dropper, stressing who they know in the company
- No sense of humor

If you recognize any of these characteristics as a possible problem area in your interview style, take steps to correct it.

WHAT! I DON'T WANT THE JOB

Although it's best to know in advance of the interview that you want the job, there will likely be occasions during your career when you realize, either in the meeting or upon reflection, that the job isn't for you. If it is absolutely clear during the interview that the job is just impossible - a sudden revelation of lots of overtime or travel expectations that conflict with your personal life, the salary range is emphatically non-negotiable and nowhere near your acceptable range, the culture of that organization doesn't fit with your own values - be honest and take yourself out of the running. This takes tact and diplomacy. Stress it is the position, not the organization, that is not right for you. Graciously thank the interviewer for the opportunity to interview. Stringing a company along because you don't like to say no is unfair.

If you were undecided during the interview but become convinced the opportunity isn't for you after evaluating it, immediately write a gracious letter withdrawing your name from consideration. Again thank the interviewer for the opportunity and emphasize that it is the timing, the position - whatever your valid reason - and not the company itself.

APPENDIX ONE

QUESTIONS, QUESTIONS AND MORE QUESTIONS

Here are another 100 questions ranging from the most general to the very particular. Read them over and pay particular attention to any that make you feel uncomfortable. Don't be put on the spot at the interview. Anticipate and have your answers ready.

About you

- How would you rate yourself as a employee on a scale of one to ten?
- Are you a happy person?
- What do you worry about?
- How do you deal with rejection?
- Are you a natural leader or natural follower?
- Are you interested in sports?
- How have you shown initiative?
- Are you a risk-taker or someone who plays it safe?
- If you could change one thing about your personality, what would it be?
- What do you like to do with your spare time?
- What is your best personality trait?
- What is your worst personality trait?
- How would you work with someone you don't like?
- What are your personal long-term goals?
- What are your personal short-term goals?
- How well do you work under pressure?
- How are you upgrading your skills?
- What would you do if money was not a concern?
- What's your favorite book or TV show?
- How would your co-workers describe you?
- How do you deal with criticism?
- Do you like working with numbers?
- Do you like working with computers?

- Do you like working with people?
- Do you like working?

About your skills
- What's the toughest problem you've ever solved?
- How do you deal with failure?
- How effective are you under pressure?
- Are you willing to take risks?
- Do you pay attention to details?
- Do you prefer to work alone or with others?
- What decisions are difficult for you?
- What skills do you think you need to improve?
- What have you learned from your current job?
- Are you an innovator?
- Can you think strategically?
- What were the results of your last performance appraisal?
- How do you organize your time?
- How would you handle an angry customer?
- How would you help a co-worker with a personal problem?
- What would you do if some team members weren't doing their share of the work?
- Which languages are you fluent in?
- What skills do you think the position requires?
- What experience do you have in making oral presentations?
- Have you handled fiscal responsibilities?
- Can you work alone?
- Can you work without direct supervision?
- In what ways did you prepare for this interview?
- I need another copy of your résumé. Do you have one with you?
- How would you evaluate my interviewing skills?

About your experience
- What work experience has helped you the most?
- Besides your education, what other areas of preparation do you have for this position?
- You've had little experience in this field. How do you intend to learn?

- Tell me about your work experience. What are your responsibilities?
- Why did you choose this field to study?
- What criticism has helped you the most? Who was it from?
- Has your work experience prepared you for this position?
- How would you evaluate your present employer's strengths?
- How would you evaluate your present employer's weaknesses?
- Can you give me an example of one of your failures?
- What leadership positions have you held?
- Have you any experience working to deadlines?
- Did you have any problems in your previous job?
- During school, what did you do with your summers?
- How do you complete a boring job?
- How do you do your most interesting job task?
- Can you describe a typical day at your last job?
- How many hours do you typically work each week?
- What have been your greatest accomplishments?
- Why did you leave your last job?
- Are you still employed?
- How do you interview while still employed?
- Does your current employer know that you're interviewing for another job?
- May we contact your employer?
- Why do you want to leave your current job if you like it so much?

Now the details
- Why are you interested in our company?
- What kind of a job are you looking for?
- What challenges are you looking for in a job?
- Are you willing to relocate or travel?
- Are you looking for a permanent job?
- Do you have a problem with routine tasks?
- How long would it take you to start contributing to our company?
- What do you find most interesting about this job?
- What do you find least interesting about this job?
- Where do you see yourself in 10 years?

- What do you know about our company?
- This is a much smaller/larger company than you have ever worked for. How do you feel about that?
- What do you feel would be an acceptable attendance record?
- What can you bring to this company?
- What position are you interested in?
- Our company has a mission statement. Do you have a personal mission statement? What is it?
- What do you know about our competitors?
- How long are you going to stay with the company?
- How much business will you attract to our company in the next months/years?
- How do you feel about working on the weekends?
- How much overtime could you work?
- Do you mind going on training courses on weekends?
- Which do you consider more valuable: a high salary or job recognition and advancement opportunities?
- Have you seen our Web site?

JOB INTERVIEW FOLLOW-UP FORM

Print up several copies of a follow-up form. Customize it to be most helpful for you. Remember to take one along to an interview and take the time directly after the interview to record your impressions and any follow-ups. For example, perhaps you mentioned an article in a trade publication and the interviewer expressed an interest in reading it. Note down to photocopy it and enclose it with your thank-you note. Make sure to give yourself enough information for the form to be useful for review purposes. Write down both positive and negative comments about your performance in the interview. "I remembered to recap my three top skills in my closing statement. But, yuck, I realize I did that nervous giggle." Learn from your own mistakes. Review these personal performance reports before the next interview to remind yourself of any mistakes you don't want to repeat.

Company name _____

Address _____

Phone _____

Fax _____

E-mail _____

Date of interview _____

Name/title of interviewer(s) _____

Job description _____

Outfit worn _____

Follow-up information to be sent _____

Positive/negative aspects of your performance _____

Other comments (ie., dress code) _____

_____

Status

Thank-you letter sent _____

References contacted and briefed _____

Telephone follow-up made _____

Result _____

OVER 100 CLASSIC COLES NOTES ARE ALSO AVAILABLE: